A Practical
Guide to
Buying and
Renting

Your First Home

The Lifeplanner Series

The Lifeplanner series addresses personal finance and consumer issues in a jargon-free, readable way, taking the fear out of planning your life. So whether you are thinking about buying a house, having a baby, gettting married or planning your retirement, the Lifeplanner series will help you do so wisely.

Titles available are:

Balancing Your Career, Family and Life
Getting Married
Landing Your First Job
Making the Most of Being a Student
Making the Most of Retirement
The Young Professional's Guide to Personal Finance
Your Child's Education
Your First Home: A Practical Guide to Buying and Renting
Your First Investment Portfolio

Available from all good booksellers. For further information on the series, please contact:

Kogan Page
120 Pentonville Road
London
N1 9JN
Tel: 0171 278 0433
Fax: 0171 837 6348
e-mail: kpinfo@kogan-page.co.uk
or visit our website: www.Kogan-page.co.uk

The Daily Telegraph
LIFEPLANNER

A Practical
Guide to
Buying and
Renting
Your
First
Home

2nd Edition

Niki
Chesworth

KOGAN
PAGE

First published in 1998
Second edition, 1999

Kogan Page Limited
120 Pentonville Road
London N1 9JN

British Library Cataloguing in Publication Data

A CIP record for this book is available from the British Library.

ISBN 0 7494 3184 9

Typeset by Kogan Page
Printed and bound in Great Britain by Thanet Press Ltd, Margate

Contents

Contents

Jali Ltd

Jali Ltd was started in 1990 and has grown considerably every year since then. Originally concentrating on bespoke fretwork panels and sheets for shopfitting, restaurant and leisure purposes, Jali soon began to attract the attention of home interest journalists.

Jali screens and panels were featured in various journals and at exhibitions. The response was so great that the Jali Home Decoration Range was designed to make sure that anyone could easily use Jali fretwork in their home.

The Home Decoration Range is a range of decorative products including shelving, pelmets trellis and cupboards, all made from easy to use MDF. The range is ideal for home improvement, whether for a small project or to completely transform a room.

A new brochure has recently been launched to include a fuller range than at first and includes many new products, such as fretwork arches, animals and freestanding screens.

At first there was nowhere to buy Jali products, so everything was sold via Mail Order. Jali started to look for retail stockists to stock Jali products and stockists were keen to take the Jali products that were so successful by Mail Order. Soon Jali products were in many independent retailers and small retail chains throughout the country.

When the Home Decoration Range proved to be such a success, it was followed in 1995 by a new idea, Jali "Made to Measure" Radiator Cabinets.

Jali Made to Measure Radiator Cabinets are the most popular Jali product yet! They are made to each customer's own sizes and are sold as flat pack DIY kits.

As Jali Radiator Cabinets are inexpensive, they are a good solution. They can be made to fit any specific situation, whether in an alcove, against a wall or even to be incorporated into a bookcase or a cupboard.

You can now buy Jali Home Decoration and Radiator Cabinets directly via Mail Order, through over sixty Focus Do It All branches and one hundred and fifty independent retailers. There is a list available from Jali, as the retailers are increasing every month!

In 1997, Jali won the first of many awards, Kent Business Awards "Small Business Award". Since then they have won many other accolades, including Nicholas Showan, Managing Director of Jali Ltd, winning Kent Businessman of the Year in 1998.

Jali are still manufacturing bespoke fretworks for many clients, including work for tv, film and major retailers. You have probably seen Jali in a shop window or in a film without realising!

The BBC programmes "Homefront", "Changing Rooms" and "Change That" have all recently featured Jali and Jali fretwork has been used at various film studios in the feature films "Elizabeth", "Shakespeare in Love" and "The Mummy". Currently they are working on the sequel to "101 Dalmations" for Shepperton Studios and the next film to be released including Jali fretwork is the new James Bond film, "The World is Not Enough"!

Jali have also worked extensively on fretwork for "Fantasy Rooms", Laurence Llewelyn-Bowen's latest series and in the accompanying book, which is currently sold out and being reprinted.

Jali brochures are available free of charge for the Specifier Range, the Made to Measure Radiator Cabinets and for the Home Decoration Range. Please contact us with any questions or further information at:

Jali Ltd, Albion Works, Church Lane, Barham,
Canterbury, Kent CT4 6QS
Tel: 01227 831710 Fax: 01227 831950
Or visit our new website at www.jali.co.uk

The Daily Telegraph

The Young Professional's Guide to Personal Finance
Niki Chesworth

MONEY: we argue over it, worry about it, and when we are not earning it we are spending it. Yet few find time to make the most of it.

A young professional is likely to spend 100,000 hours earning during their working life and can expect to be paid upwards of £2 million. Even though it may be a struggle financially at the start, in the future a professional can expect to buy two or three homes, invest for a rainy day, build up a pension and – by the time retirement age comes – be reasonably wealthy.

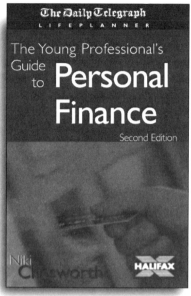

The last thing that a young professional climbing the career ladder wants to think about is being made redundant, saving for the future or retirement. But failing to manage finances now – taking out insurance, picking the right mortgage, pension and investments – could prove very costly in the future.

This new book is aimed at young professionals – people with potentially high earnings who spend so much time working, they don't have time to make their money work. Written with a minimum amount of jargon and the maximum amount of practical advice, *The Young Professional's Guide to Personal Finance* is the most comprehensive source of information available. And the sooner it is read, the sooner money will be saved!

CONTENTS:
- Managing Your Money
- Banking
- Borrowing
- Saving
- Investment Advice
- Investing
- Pensions
- Mortgages
- Insurance
- Tax
- Complaining and the Law
- Wills

£6.99 • Paperback • ISBN 0 7494 3002 8 • 224 pages • 1999

KOGAN PAGE
120 Pentonville Road, London N1 9JN
Tel: 0171 278 0433 • Fax: 0171 837 6348 • www.kogan-page.co.uk

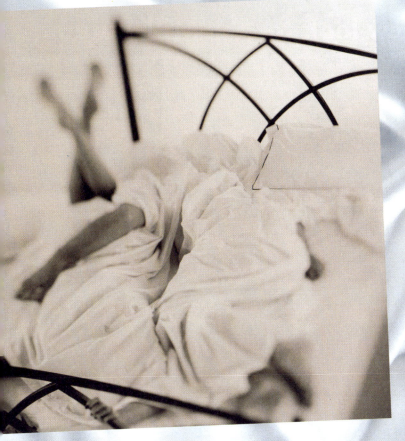

Want to treat your home to a new look for the Millennium?

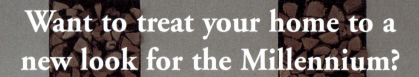

Kährs wood floors - a beautiful investment for the future.

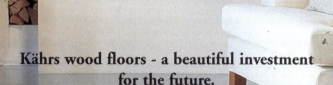

Introduction

Are we heading for another property crash? There is a concern that recent rampant house price inflation in parts of the UK – which has seen prices up 30 per cent over the year in some areas – could lead to a slump on a scale unseen since the late 1980s and early 1990s.

Buyers are tripping over themselves to buy properties with up to 11 after each home for sale in the South East.

Gazumping – whereby another buyer outbids you at the last minute – is rife once again and new housing developments are being sold before they have even been built.

However, that is where the similarities end. Interest rates are expected to remain relatively low and mortgages, at the time of writing, were still at their cheapest level for 30 years. Back in the early 1990s interest rates peaked at 15 per cent – almost three times their current level.

Affordability remains excellent, with the proportion of income needed to finance house purchase around 15 per cent, compared with in excess of 25 per cent at the height of the 1980s boom.

In addition, unemployment is low so there is less of a risk that homebuyers will be repossessed because they cannot meet their monthly mortgage bills. Record repossessions were partly to blame for the last downward spiral in house prices – properties were being sold at any price by borrowers desperate to get off the property ladder.

Also the property market is not overheating. In real terms prices in the summer of 1999 were still 7 per cent below their long-term trend and about 20 per cent below their 1989 peak according to the Nationwide.

So although prices have risen by around 40 per cent since their trough in 1995, we are still quite some way from boom conditions.

The housing market is also very different for the first-time buyer of the millennium.

That is why this book looks not just at buying but also renting. First-time buyers are leaving it later and later to get on to the property ladder. This is partly because house price inflation means that most find they cannot afford to get on to the first rung of the property ladder – particularly if they have left university with a mountain of debts. So a first home for most is a rented flat.

However, the bulk of the book is still dedicated to home buying. For owning a home is part of our culture with almost seven in ten households owner-occupied. Of the remaining three in ten, most want to become homeowners in the future.

So while 24 per cent of those aged under 24 and 57 per cent of those aged 25 to 34 are already buying a property with a mortgage, most of those that have yet to take on the responsibility of a home loan and to enjoy the benefits of ownership plan to do so in the future.

Written in plain English, this book not only tells you how to rent or buy, but how to overcome the problems, reduce the costs and avoid unnecessary pitfalls.

Should You Rent or Buy?

Often this is not a straightforward 'either or' option. Few have sufficient capital and income to buy their first property: instead, they rent their first home while they save up a deposit and decide where they want to make their permanent home.

The other factor boosting the demand for rented accommodation is changing work patterns. Increasingly, workers are on short-term contracts and as such may find it difficult to take out a mortgage. Younger workers also tend to job-hop as they move up the career ladder and may not want to be tied down to a particular geographical area. And, of course, they are often still saddled with student debts and loans. This has led to an increase in the average age of first-time buyers by three years since the peak of the 1980s' property boom to 27.

At the same time, legislation to protect landlords from sitting tenants has increased the supply of good quality rental accommodation. Increasingly, private individuals are buying properties as an investment with a view to renting them – usually for far more than the monthly mortgage costs. As a result, not only are these properties new or in good condition but the standard and quality of furnishings is high to maximize the rents.

You can tell how popular renting has become by the number of estate agents that now offer as many – or more – properties for rent as they do for sale.

However, the number of those renting is still a fraction of the number of people buying their own home. The UK already has one of the highest levels of homeownership in the world with 67 per cent of households owner-occupied. We don't have sayings like 'an Englishman's home is his castle' in our language for nothing.

It is not just desire to own a home – particularly at a time when prices are increasing – that is encouraging first-time buyers. They are also motivated by the fear that if they fail to buy now – when the average house already costs more than three times the average salary – they will find that prices will rise even further, putting homeownership out of their reach.

The Cost Comparison

Although renting is seen as the easy and cheap alternative to buying, it can be as expensive – if not more so. Landlords buy with the aim of renting out the property for more than the mortgage or financing costs of buying the home. As a result, you will usually pay more in rent than you would in mortgage repayments to purchase the same property. It has made renting a flat in London more expensive than in either Paris or New York.

However, those who rent do not have the expense of long-term maintenance, finding the deposit, insuring the property, furnishing and decorating it or paying to find tenants. And there is no risk involved. Renters do not have to bear the brunt of sharp increases in interest rates or worry that the property will be left vacant for several months or that tenants will not pay the rent.

But while there is no risk in renting, there is also no reward. As the saying goes 'Rent money is dead money'. Those who buy will, after 25 years or so, own their property outright and will – if past trends continue – see substantial capital appreciation. Those who rent will have to keep paying rent forever and will never have the freedom of owning a substantial asset.

As a result, over the longer term you are likely to pay more in rent than you would in mortgage repayments. While your mortgage repayments may seem high initially, over the long run your salary will usually increase and inflation will reduce the cost of repayments in real terms. So after five or ten years your mortgage payments will take up a smaller proportion of your income. Rents, on the other hand, rise and as a result will generally take up the same proportion of your income.

Who Should Rent?

Although most people want to buy their own home, for some it is not practical or advisable. These include:

▌ Those who cannot afford to get on to the property ladder (either because their salary is not large enough or they do not have a lump sum to cover the costs/deposit).

▌ Those who want to buy, but would rather save up a deposit first (those with larger deposits generally qualify for cheaper mortgages).

▌ Those who have uncertain income and cannot commit to regular mortgage payments.

▌ Those who do not have a permanent job but are on a fixed contract (these people can find it harder to qualify for a mortgage and, if they do, the mortgage rate may be higher).

▌ Those who expect to move home in the near future or want the flexibility to move towns/cities for employment purposes.

▌ Those who do not yet want the responsibility of owning a property (for instance they are working too hard to want to spend time decorating and furnishing a home).

▌ Those who fear they may lose their job in the near future. If you are unemployed your rent will usually be paid for you by Social Security provided it is a reasonable rent for the area you are living in and you are over 25. If you buy a home you may not receive any help from Social Security to meet your mortgage interest payments for the first nine months. So unless you have mortgage protection insurance – and even if you have insurance it may not pay out if you claim shortly after taking out the policy – you may risk losing your home.

Who Should Buy?

▌ Those with a regular income who will – if they take out the best value mortgage – often find they can buy more cheaply than they can rent.

▌ Those who are established in an area and expect to live and work there for the next few years.

▌ Those who are prepared to take on the responsibility of home-ownership – maintenance, repairs, a commitment to meet monthly mortgage payments, etc.

▌ Those wanting the freedom of homeownership – being able to decorate their home as they wish and not having a landlord breathing down their necks.

▌ Those wanting to cut their housing costs – for instance by renting out rooms so that their monthly mortgage bills are far lower than the rent on a similar property.

Pros and Cons of Renting

Pros:	Cons:
You do not need a large deposit.	No capital appreciation.
	It is not *your* home.
Flexibility to move.	
	You may have to move after
No responsibility for maintenance/repairs/ redecoration.	six months/a year, particularly if the property is let on a shorthold tenancy.

Pros:

You can often rent a nicer property than you could afford to buy because lenders restrict the amount you can borrow, whereas landlords only want to know that you can afford the rent.

If you run into financial difficulties you can easily move to cheaper accommodation.

Cons:

When you renew your tenancy or rents are reviewed, your rent may increase or the property may no longer be affordable.

If you delay buying you may find that prices have increased so much you can no longer afford to buy.

Pros and Cons of Buying

Pros:

It is *your* home, you can decorate it as you wish and do not have the problem of dealing with a landlord.

You, not a landlord, can decide when you want to move.

Once you have repaid your mortgage you will no longer have to pay to live in the property (unlike renters) and should own a substantial asset.

Mortgage repayments can be cheaper than rent and if you get into financial difficulties you can rent out a room to help pay the mortgage.

Cons:

It is a major responsibility and a financial drain as you have to pay for maintenance/repairs.

If mortgage rates rise and house prices fall you may not be able to pay your mortgage/ may be unable to sell as your mortgage debt is greater than the value of the property.

If you cannot pay your mortgage your home may be repossessed and you will find it difficult to obtain mortgage finance in the future.

Part 1 Renting

1 What is Available and Affordable?

What Type of Accommodation?

Your choice will depend largely on how much you can afford. The options are:

- renting a room/becoming a lodger

- sharing a flat or house with friends

- taking out a tenancy/lease on a flat or house

Furnished or Unfurnished?

The decision will generally depend on whether or not you have a substantial amount of furniture. If you don't have many belongings a furnished property is likely to be the cheapest and easiest option.

The demand for unfurnished accommodation has increased in recent years, but most of this has come from families who intend to rent for a long period and want to establish their own home. As a result the rents on unfurnished properties tend to be higher.

At the same time new fire regulations have made it preferable for landlords to rent unfurnished properties as they can no longer furnish homes with second-hand furniture or old cast offs. Another factor influencing the increased availability of unfurnished accommodation is that landlords now have more protection against sitting tenants. In the past landlords were advised to furnish property to avoid this risk, but now there is no legal distinction between furnished and unfurnished accommodation.

Stamp Duty

Under the Stamp Duty Act, technically tenants have to pay 1 per cent of the annual rent (or part thereof if the property is let for less than a year) if the property is unfurnished. Furnished property carries a stamp duty of just £1 provided the tenancy is for less than a year. Furnished lettings for longer than 12 months attract stamp duty at 1 per cent. However, in practice this rarely happens and even if the tenancy agreement is unstamped the contract is still valid.

Finding Somewhere to Rent

Friends and Family

This is usually the easiest way to find a room to rent. However, make sure you have an agreement to protect yourself should you fall out and then be asked to leave with little or no notice. To save arguments at a later date, agree (preferably in writing) what you do and do not have to pay for.

Becoming a Lodger

The days when renting a room in a house or flat was a bit like joining the cast of *Rising Damp* are long over. The government's Rent-A-Room scheme, which allows homeowners to rent out one room in their home tax free provided the rent is not more than £4250 a year (for the 1999/2000 tax year), means that an increasing number of rooms are being rented out. The advantage is that the owner can only rent out one room under this scheme so you will not be living in a house full of bedsits. Also, because the owner must live in the property it will generally be furnished to a good standard and be well maintained.

Flat Share Services

These tend to be targeted at young people, so the advantage is that you are likely to be sharing with people of a similar age. However, remember you will be living in close proximity to strangers and this can cause problems, particularly if one sharer is particularly noisy, fails to pay his or her rent on time, leaves a mess or makes a habit of eating your food. If the other sharers want to move out you could be left with the responsibility for paying the entire rent or for advertising for new flatmates. If you cannot find new sharers or afford the rent, you may be forced to move out.

The advantages of sharing with someone who owns the property are that they will take responsibility for maintenance and repairs and will be more approachable than some faceless landlord. However, if the owner lives in the property he or she is likely to be more fussy about cleanliness and noise and you may feel it is their home, not yours.

Newspaper/Magazine Advertisements

These often offer relatively cheap accommodation (unless the advertisement is placed by a letting agent). Make sure you have a formal tenancy agreement to protect you from rogue landlords. Renting directly from the landlord will often mean that you will have a more personal relationship. This can be a disadvantage or an advantage depending on the personalities involved.

The Jargon

When looking through classified advertising it may be difficult to decipher the terminology:

apt	apartment	gdn	garden
c/h	central heating	hs	house
dbl,db	double	lge	large
ff	fully furnished	n/s	non-smoker
f/ft	fully fitted	pkg	parking
fl,flt	flat	prof	professional
gge	garage	sgl	single
sh	shared, as in sh kit	shwr	shower
	and bath (shared	spac	spacious
	kitchen and bathroom)		

> **Warning:** Be careful when responding to newspaper adver-
> tisements. If you are a single woman take a friend along
> when you view the property. Do not part with any money on
> the spot, however desperate you are to rent the property. It
> has been known for crooks to show tenants round flats and
> then demand the deposit and first month's rent in cash, only
> to disappear before the tenant realizes that the bogus land-
> lord does not own the property.

Housing Associations

This accommodation is usually restricted to those who meet the
criteria of the association – which often means you have to be
homeless or spend months or even years on a waiting list.

Developers/Property Companies

Some property developers and other residential investment companies are now building new homes for rent rather than sale. The
advantages of these are that the properties are brand new or only a
few years old and as such should be in good condition.

Letting Agents

You will be required to pay an administration fee. In return you
should find that the landlord is reputable, your deposit is protected
as it is held in a bank account controlled by the letting agent and the
agent will have a legally prepared tenancy agreement. If you are
using a reputable company (for instance, a member of the
Association of Residential Letting Agents) you should not have
to pay introductory fees or fees for being listed on the agent's
books, but you will have to pay for inventories, administration,
preparation of the tenancy agreement and for the agent to take up
references.

Many established firms are members of the Association of Residential Lettings Agents (01494 431 680) which produces a free

leaflet for landlords and tenants called *Troublefree letting – what every landlord and tenant should ask.*

Warning: Letting agents should not charge you just for registering on their books. However, some do charge a 'holding deposit' from tenants, which is paid once a suitable property is found. This charge can range from £50 to £200. If you have to pull out of the tenancy the deposit will usually be kept by the agent. A few do not return this holding deposit even if the tenancy goes ahead. So always check what charges will be made, get a signed receipt and ask for any terms and conditions to be put in writing.

Budgeting for the Costs

Although the initial costs involved in renting are far lower than buying, you will often still require a lump sum of at least £1000.

The Deposit

You will usually be required to pay a deposit of between one month and six weeks' rent. This deposit covers the landlord against damage to the property or fixtures and fittings as well as the cost of returning the property to the state in which it was rented to you.

Rent in Advance

In addition to the deposit, you will also be required to pay a month's rent in advance. Landlords often require standing orders for payment of the rent to ensure that it is paid on time. If you don't pay by standing order or direct debit make sure you have a rent/receipt book.

Also note that some tenancy agreements give the landlord the right to charge interest on late payment of rent.

Agent's Fees

If you are using a letting agent the administration fees should have been agreed in advance. Fees are often in the region of £100 to £150. Remember, VAT is added to fees. If you have taken out a tenancy for only a short period of time (for instance, six months) and then want to renew the agreement you will then have to pay a second lot of fees to extend the tenancy (although these should not be as high as the fees to cover the initial agreement).

Costs after You Have Moved In

You should not forget to budget for additional costs once you have moved in. Some of these – such as insurance – may have to be paid as soon as you move and at a time when you may be struggling financially after paying for the deposit and a month's rent in advance.

- You will generally have to pay your own council tax as this will not be included in the rent.

- It will usually be your responsibility to obtain a TV licence – even if the landlord provides a television in the property – unless you are a lodger.

- Gas and electricity bills (although the landlord normally pays the water rates).

- You will be responsible for telephone bills – and any connection fees.

- You need to take out insurance for your own contents/ possessions.

Viewing a Property

When you purchase a home you view the property several times, arrange a survey and make detailed checks from whether the central heating works to whether there is any damp. But most of those renting a flat usually make their decision after only a brief five-minute inspection.

Remember you are making a commitment to rent for a certain period of time (notice in the first few months is often 12 weeks) so if, after moving in, you find the property is not suitable you will be forced to live there for several months.

The reason why it is essential to inspect the property carefully is that you are agreeing to take on that property 'as seen'. Landlords do not have to change or alter the property, fixtures or furnishings once the tenancy has started. They only have to repair or replace items that are broken or no longer work properly. So if the central heating is inadequate in the depths of winter, you will have to tolerate the cold. The landlord does not have to install additional radiators and is only responsible for ensuring the central heating works properly and is safe.

Remember, letting agents represent the landlord, not the tenant, even though you are paying them a fee. So the agent is unlikely to tell you that the flat is draughty, cold, the water pressure is low or that the neighbours are noisy. You have to find out these things for yourself.

For longer tenancy agreements, particularly of older houses, a survey may be a worthwhile investment so that any problems can be written into the contract or repair or replacement arranged before the tenancy begins. This is particularly important if you are taking on a 'self-repairing' lease which puts the responsibility for maintenance and repairs on to the tenant.

Before viewing a property for rent you will probably have already ascertained that the flat/house meets your requirements including:

▌ rent – is it affordable/within your budget?

▌ size – either the whole property or your room and the total size of the property if you are sharing

▌ location – near to or within easy travelling distance from work.

The initial inspection/viewing should tell you instantly if the property is suitable. Check:

▊ the quality of decor

▊ the quality of furniture, fixtures and fittings

▊ what items are included/what items will be removed before you start to rent – such as the washing machine, dishwasher, kettle, TV, pictures, rugs, garden furniture. You don't want to move in and find that much of the furniture or fittings have been taken away by the previous tenant or by the landlord.

It is often at this stage that tenants agree to rent a property. But you do need to make additional investigations. Before agreeing to rent a property check the following by inspecting the flat or by asking the landlord or letting agent:

▊ Security: adequate locks, outside lighting, solid front door, etc.

▊ Safety: smoke alarms, fire exits, whether gas appliances have been maintained correctly and that furniture meets safety standards.

▊ Ventilation: will the bathroom or kitchen steam up because there are no windows?

▊ Extra costs: council tax can be expensive in some areas. Check the usual costs of heating and electricity – inefficient systems cost more.

▊ Insurance: the landlord usually arranges insurance for fixtures and furnishings that are provided with the flat, but what about your own belongings? Insurance can be expensive in some areas. Check the landlord's policy to find out what is covered and what you are liable for.

▊ Heating: how is the property heated, how does the system work and has it been serviced recently?

▊ Water: check the system by running taps, flushing the toilet and testing the shower for water pressure.

▌ Wiring: check that this is safe (it is not an obvious DIY job). Also check the number of electrical points.

▌ Test the furniture and fittings. You may find that the sofa has loose springs, the bed is about to collapse or there is a wobbly chair. All these should be noted on the inventory or you may be liable to replace or repair them when you leave the property.

▌ Rules: are there rules about pets, parties and noise levels after a certain hour?

▌ Your own possessions: are you allowed to put up your own pictures, bring in your own furniture?

▌ Decor: are you allowed to redecorate (this will apply particularly to those renting cheaper properties with poor decor or those planning to rent a property for a considerable amount of time)?

▌ Does the landlord have permission to sub-let? You may be renting from someone who does not have the right to rent out the property.

Then make the following additional checks by viewing the property at different times and finding out as much as possible about the area:

▌ Noise – if you are viewing at a weekend you may be unaware that during the week the area is very noisy or you may find that you have noisy or undesirable neighbours.

▌ Transport – not only the distance to and from local transport facilities but the reliability and quality of service of buses, trains or tubes.

▌ Local facilities – if you work long hours you don't want to return to your new home only to find that there are no shops open.

■ Parking – if you have a car, make sure that you will be able to park it, that you will qualify for a resident's parking permit or that it is safe to leave your car parked on the street.

Remember, it is your responsibility to check and double check. For instance, the advertisement may say parking is available. If you don't view the parking space you may not realize that it is too small to park your car in or that the car park is several hundred yards away.

THINK LOCAL - THINK MUTUAL - THINK 'MANSFIELD'

Paul Barton of The Mansfield Building Society explains:

The objectives of the small building society remain as valid as they were when the movement started over 200 years ago.

To provide the best possible return to savers and charge the lowest possible lending rate remains the key philosophy.

Sufficient profit is generated to ensure investor protection for members whilst providing resource to develop new and improved services and products.

Having no accountability to third party shareholders means that societies, like The Mansfield, are able to provide value to savers and borrowers alike.

Borrowers may be surprised to discover that independent research consistently shows that small societies often charge less interest over ten years on a typical interest only, standard rate mortgage than the larger, better known high street plc lenders.

The culture of the smaller society is more focused to the member's needs, and is committed to offer the best possible products and services, but with a more personal approach.

Don't be put off the smaller lender simply because that may not provide the 'one stop' approach of the bigger lenders - they know that home buyers, and in particular first time buyers, want value for money - but they know that it's much better to get personal services as well!

2 Rental Agreements and Deposits

Rental Agreements

Once you have found a property that suits your needs and meets your requirements you should then examine the rental agreement to make sure you are happy with the terms and conditions it imposes.

If you are planning to rent a flat or house in most cases you will usually have to take out a 'shorthold tenancy' and sign a tenancy agreement. This protects the landlord from sitting tenants.

Tenancies usually run for an initial period of six months, after which they may be renewable. The new Housing Act introduced in the spring of 1997 means that assured shorthold tenancies no longer need to last for a minimum period of six months. However, most still do.

For those wanting to rent for longer periods there is an 'assured longhold tenancy' agreement.

Most tenancy agreements comply with the Housing Act, although the exact wording can vary from agent to agent, with some letting agents inserting extra clauses to cover specific aspects of the property or area. If you are renting directly from a landlord, he or she will usually use a standard printed agreement bought from a legal stationers.

Remember, the tenancy agreement is a legally binding document between you and the landlord and as such you should read it carefully before signing. It should state:

▌ the address of the property;

▌ the amount of rent and to whom it is payable;

▌ length/term of tenancy;

▌ when rent is payable and what it includes/excludes;

▌ your rights and responsibilities (from a ban on pets to a requirement to leave the property clean at the end of the tenancy);

▌ the amount of the deposit and to whom it is payable;

▌ notice periods that both you and the landlord must give to ter-
minate the agreement;

▌ bills that you are responsible for (for instance council tax/
gas/electricity/telephone/TV licence);

▌ there may also be security requirements. For instance you may
be required to ensure that the property is left secure at all
times. You may also be required to give the person managing
the property written notice if you plan to be away from the
property for more than seven, 14 or 30 days;

▌ you may also be told that you cannot change the locks or install
any additional ones without the written consent of the landlord;

▌ there will usually be numerous other conditions which you
should read carefully.

Rental agreements often stipulate that the landlord can enter and
take possession of the property if you breach your tenancy agreement. However, landlords must usually apply to the courts before
doing so.

Some agreements also state that the landlord is not liable for any
injury suffered by tenants, even if this is caused by a defect on the
premises or by neglect. However, tenants can normally make a
civil claim against the landlord if, for instance, they are injured as a
result of faulty wiring or a dangerous gas boiler.

When you sign your tenancy agreement you may also have to sign a 'Notice Requiring Possession (Assured Shorthold Tenancy)' or a 'Recovery of Possession of Dwelling' form which gives advance notice that you will vacate the property on a set date when the tenancy ends. Under the Housing Act this form protects the landlord and means that should the tenant fail to leave on the stated date or fail to pay the rent a court order for possession can be obtained more quickly.

When you sign the agreement you will usually be required to have your signature witnessed before an independent witness who should sign giving his or her name, address and occupation.

References

Landlords usually require references to ensure that you are who you say you are and can afford to pay the rent. As a result the landlord or letting agent may ask your permission to contact your bank or employer. You may also be asked to provide references from current and previous landlords. Not all landlords check references, but you should be prepared for them to do so and as such should make sure you alert all referees.

If you are using a professional letting agent you should expect them to conduct more thorough checks on prospective tenants.

If you are using a letting agent then that agent will usually write to your bank or building society to confirm your ability to meet the rental commitment. They may also ask if they can contact your employer. Agents may also check your credit rating with a credit reference agency to find out if you have any county court judgements against you for non-payment of debts.

It is essential that you are honest as the new Housing Act introduced in early 1997 allows landlords to evict tenants who gain a tenancy by knowingly providing false information.

Making Your Own Checks

You may not want to go as far as asking your landlord for references, but you should still undertake your own checks. It has been known for landlords to rent out property when they are not entitled to do so. For instance, they may be in default on their rent/mortgage, may not be the legal tenant of the property or may not have permission to sub-let. You could hand over the deposit and first month's rent only to find that the property is about to be repossessed.

Deposits

In most cases you will be required to pay between a month and six weeks' rent as a deposit to cover any damage to the property or the furniture, fixtures and fittings. The deposit also covers any costs incurred by the landlord to clean or make good the property after the tenancy ends. The deposit is not refundable until you vacate – or for two to three weeks after you leave – the property. The delay may be while the landlord gets estimates for or pays for repairs, replacement of items or for cleaning.

If you are renting through a reputable letting agent, the deposit will normally be held in an account run by the agent. You will need to make sure that the money is protected in case the agent goes bust or absconds with your money. If you are giving the deposit directly to the landlord there may be even less protection. To avoid losing your deposit ask the following questions:

If using a letting agent or estate agent:

▌ Will the deposit be held in a separate account?

▌ Can the agent get access to funds held in that account or is the money protected in any way?

▌ Does the agent require the signature of both the tenant and the landlord to release the deposit? This will prevent the landlord from keeping your deposit at the end of the tenancy.

Letting agents do not have to hold deposits in a separate account unless they are members of a trade body (such as the Association of Residential Letting Agents). Check first – not all letting agents are professional.

If paying a deposit to a landlord:

▌ Where will the deposit be held? If it is in the landlord's bank account you may have difficulty in getting it returned and certainly won't earn interest. Occasionally landlords open a separate account and give the tenant the interest at the end of the tenancy. But this is very rare.

▌ Will the landlord allow you to open a joint account that requires both the landlord's and the tenant's signature before the money can be withdrawn? This way neither you nor the landlord can get access to the deposit without mutual agreement. And if you open an interest-bearing account you can split the interest.

Always make sure you are given a receipt for your deposit to prove you have made the payment. Keep a note of who you paid the deposit to and when.

Warning: One of the most common problems faced by renters is getting their deposit returned at the end of the tenancy. Landlords usually claim they have good reason to withhold the deposit, often saying that the money was used to pay for cleaning of the property or damage to furniture and carpets. When you leave the property you should check through the inventory with either the landlord or a specialist agency employed by the landlord and agree what level of repairs/cleaning needs to be done. Then, if there is a dispute, you have written proof of what was agreed.

Making the Payments

In cases where payment of the first month's rent and the deposit is required quickly you will have to pay either by cash or by banker's draft. Always make sure you receive a receipt as proof of payment.

3 Moving In

You can usually move in at 12 noon: the same time applies to vacating the property. Prior to moving into a property you should notify the following:

▌ The relevant utility services – they should be told of a change of occupier and you should ask for the meters to be read. This is so that you are not charged for outstanding bills or for any electricity or gas used prior to the date that you move in.

▌ Your bank, building society, tax office and any other savings and investment companies.

▌ Your employer.

▌ The Post Office – if you want mail forwarded from a previous address.

▌ The council, so that you can start paying council tax.

▌ The TV licensing authority.

▌ British Telecom – or other telephone service provider.

▌ A local doctor/dentist – so you can register as a patient.

▌ The local council, if you want to apply for a parking permit.

The Inventory

If you are renting through a professional letting agent, the agent will normally employ a firm to take an inventory at the start of the tenancy and at the end. If this is not done, you should make your own list and get the landlord to sign this.

The inventory should not only include all furniture, fittings, linen, crockery and other items but should also state their condition. For instance if the carpet has stains on it, a wooden table is scratched or the curtains have not been dry cleaned, make sure a note is made of this. If you don't, when you vacate the property you may find that you are charged for cleaning the carpets and curtains or for repairing damaged furniture even though it was in this condition when you first started to rent the property.

> **Warning:** When you leave the property there will usually be a requirement that the property is thoroughly cleaned and that all items of furniture are in the same condition as at the start of the tenancy and are returned to their original location in the property. If you fail to meet these requirements you will probably be charged for cleaning or repairs and as a result the landlord may not return your deposit. If you do not have a detailed inventory you may find it hard to prove that you left the property in the same condition that you found it.

The Check-in

Make sure the inventory is checked at the time you actually move in and that both you and the landlord/landlord's agent sign the check-in report. This should include checking the inventory to ensure the contents, furniture and fixtures are as described in the inventory.

Either make sure the inventory covers the condition of the property and its contents or make out your own list and ask that the landlord/landlord's agent signs this. It should include:

▌ General condition: is it clean?

▌ Decorative order: if there are any defects, damp stains, peeling wallpaper, etc make sure this is noted or the landlord may claim that you are liable.

▌ Carpets/flooring: note if they have been cleaned or not and make a list of any marks.

▌ Curtains/upholstery: again make a note of any marks/defects and also find out if they have been cleaned before the start of the tenancy as you may be required to pay for professional cleaning before vacating the property.

▌ Furniture: note any marks, stains or scratches.

▌ Kitchen equipment: check if any items are chipped or cracked. Again, if you don't make a note of this at the start of the tenancy you may find that you are liable to replace these items when your tenancy ends. If they are part of a set you may find individual items hard to replace and may have to buy a whole new set.

▌ Lighting: check which lights are working and which are not.

▌ Glazing: make sure that there are no defects.

Meter readings: Although you will have to ask the utility companies to check meter readings when you move in, you should also get the landlord/landlord's agent to agree the meter reading at the start of the tenancy to ensure you are not charged for usage prior to the date you move in.

Keys: You should also have in writing the number of keys that you are supplied with.

Keep a copy of your check-in report along with your inventory.

4 Legal Aspects, Maintenance and Problems

Renting and the Law

Recent legislation has given more protection to landlords against sitting tenants, but has also increased the protection of tenants against unscrupulous landlords.

What Your Landlord Can and Cannot Do

Landlords cannot:

- enter a tenant's property without permission unless it is an absolute emergency

- change the locks without the tenant's permission

Landlords can:

- enter the property to inspect it or for maintenance and repairs, but only if they give reasonable notice

- require that you undertake repairs you are responsible for, and if you do not do so within the specified time period the landlord can enter the premises to make the repairs and then charge you for them

■ enter the property in the last few weeks of the tenancy to show other prospective tenants round the property

■ charge you if you fail to keep an appointment to check the inventory at the end of the tenancy

■ charge interest if you are late in paying the rent

Fire and Safety Regulations

Fire

When renting a property it is essential to check that the landlord meets all requirements for health and safety. Although there are laws in place, some unscrupulous landlords have rented out death traps in the past where faulty wiring has caused fires, a lack of fire escapes has led to the death of tenants, or faulty gas boilers have exploded.

Under the legislation, which came into force on 1 January 1997, landlords letting furnished property have to ensure that furniture has fire retardant fillings. All upholstery, fillings and covers must have passed flammability tests and be labelled accordingly. Landlords must remove 'non-compliant' furniture prior to letting or face a fine of up to £5000 or up to six months in prison. Most furniture sold since 1990 should comply, but you should ask to see fire retardant information and check the landlord has safety certificates. If the landlord is renting out his or her own home for a temporary period and not in the course of his or her business, then there is a moral rather than a legal responsibility to comply.

If the landlord fails to meet these requirements and there is a fire you may be able to make a claim for civil damages against the landlord.

New homes built after June 1992 must have smoke detectors installed on every floor.

Gas

The landlord must also ensure that a safety check of any gas appliance is carried out every 12 months by an approved person who must be CORGI registered. A record must be kept of all safety inspections and their results and this must be given to the tenant. Even if the landlord has asked for gas appliances – for instance the boiler – to be serviced this may not be sufficient as the safety check must include set information.

The regulations cover all gas appliances including mains gas, propane gas and calor gas.

Electricity

Again, the landlord must ensure that all electrical appliances and the electrical supply are safe and will not cause any danger. All new electrical appliances must carry a 'CE' mark and instruction booklets or clear working instructions must be given to tenants.

Licensing of Landlords

Many local authorities run voluntary registration schemes for landlords in their areas and these will be extended if the new legislation is introduced. It will also stop landlords holding deposits – something that causes many tenants problems as they find it hard to get them returned when they leave the property. In future – as in many cases already – the deposit will either be held in a secure account by the letting agent or in a joint account requiring the signature of both the tenant and landlord.

If you are thinking of renting find out if your local council runs one of these schemes. The new rules will require landlords to meet basic health and safety standards.

Once You Have Moved In

What You Must Do

Abide by the tenancy agreement or else you could face eviction. Your agreement may include dozens of small clauses, but you should be aware of all of them even if they only stipulate that you must weed the garden.

Some tenancy agreements go into great detail including, for example, requirements that:

▌ you do not alter the layout of the garden without the previous consent in writing of the landlord

▌ you wash all net curtains at least every six weeks

▌ you do not play any musical instruments or use any sound equipment that causes an annoyance or disturbance to adjoining residents

▌ you do not take in lodgers (so if your boyfriend/girlfriend moves in tell the landlord first)

▌ you report any faults or damage to the landlord before repairs or replacement so that the landlord can authorize the repairs or claim on his or her insurance policy

Also note that many tenancy agreements require you to inform the person managing the property should you be away from the property for more than seven consecutive days. This is not only to ensure security, but also so that the agent can check that there are no frozen pipes or other problems during your absence.

Repairs and Maintenance

If the property is managed – either by the landlord or an agent – it should mean that you do not have to worry about maintenance or ongoing repairs. However, in some cases there are a few repairs that the tenant must do.

In a legal ruling, Lord Denning put it like this:

> *'The tenant must take proper care of the premises … he must do the little jobs around the house which a reasonable tenant will do.'*

So things like changing lightbulbs, replacing fuses, day-to-day maintenance of electrical items (defrosting the fridge, keeping the washing machine clear of blockages) and unblocking the sink or drains will probably be the tenant's – not the landlord's – responsibility. If you are unsure you should make sure both you and your landlord agree in advance what management services will be provided. If you read your tenancy agreement carefully you should find that your responsibilities are explained – although this may be in 'legalese' rather than plain English.

Wear and tear clauses in most tenancy agreements require that all electrical appliances are kept in good repair by the landlord. So if the fridge or washing machine breaks down a replacement does not have to be found immediately. The landlord has 'a reasonable time' in which to arrange for repairs and no compensation for the loss of this appliance needs to be paid to the tenant.

Renting and Insurance

If you rent a furnished property you are advised to insure anything which belongs to you. If you are burgled and all that is stolen is your television, video and some cash, the insurance provided by your landlord will not cover your loss. Most tenancy agreements state that you must insure your own personal effects.

Most leases specify that the landlord's responsibility only covers the furniture and fittings. Check that it does or else you may be liable for loss of your landlord's possessions as well.

If you are renting a property, you may find that insurance is expensive or difficult to obtain. If you have difficulties, contact an insurance broker who can shop around for a suitable policy on your behalf.

Dealing with Problems

Buying a property is supposed to be one of the most stressful things in your life, along with death, divorce and redundancy.

Renting does not even make it to the top ten in the stress list. However, for some it can be a fraught process. Even if you are in the right, getting redress or compensation can be difficult. Here are the most common types of dispute and how to deal with them:

▌ The landlord refuses to sort out a problem/repair or asks you to
   sort it out, even though it is not your responsibility:

Read your tenancy agreement carefully. It will normally state that
you must inform your landlord immediately and in writing if there
is 'any damage, disrepair, defect or deficiency'. So make sure all
correspondence is in writing and you keep copies of it. Also make
sure you report problems – for instance, a leaking pipe – as soon as
possible or you may be liable for any further damage. Find out if
the problem/repair is covered by the landlord's insurance – if you
can prove it will not cost anything, the landlord is more likely to
agree to repairs.

Don't undertake any repairs yourself or pay a workman to do
them for you unless you get written permission to do so from your
landlord and an agreement that the landlord will pay the bill. It is
not unknown for landlords to not only refuse to pay for the repairs
but also to charge for leaving the premises in a poorer condition
than before because – or so they claim – the repairs were not of sufficient quality.

▌ The landlord continually pops in to check the flat/enters the
   flat when you are not there:

Most tenancy agreements stipulate that the landlord must give
you written notice before entering the property. You should point
this out without trying to antagonize the landlord. Do not change
the locks to prevent the landlord entering the flat as you will probably be in breach of your tenancy agreement.

▌ You lose your job and can no longer pay the rent:

The new Housing Act introduced in the spring of 1997 makes it easier for landlords to regain possession if you fail to pay the rent.
They can apply to the courts after only two months and claim
unpaid rent. If you get into difficulties it is essential that you claim
benefits as soon as possible. But be warned, social security will not
cover rent on a luxury apartment.

▌ The landlord refuses to return your deposit:

Either complain to the letting agent (if you used one) or threaten to take your landlord to court. Often landlords believe that they are allowed to charge you for repairs/cleaning, even though you believe you have left the property in good order and as clean as you found it.

Often the dispute is over what is 'wear and tear' and what is 'damage'. You will normally have to pay for repair or replacement of any items which have been damaged during the tenancy, but not for 'fair wear and tear'. Your landlord can tax deduct around 10 per cent of the rent to cover 'wear and tear', which covers deterioration due to normal usage. The landlord may refuse to return the deposit, claiming damage to furniture or that the property was not left in the same condition as at the start of the tenancy. If you take your case to the Small Claims Court it is vital that you have evidence – the inventory and any relevant photographs.

Some landlords keep the deposit to pay for redecoration so that they can spruce up the flat/house before new tenants move in. But if you left the flat in good decorative order and did not leave any marks on the walls or tear any wallpaper you should not have to pay for this.

If the landlord refuses to pay back the deposit, and you do not agree with his or her reasons, you may have to take out a summons in the Small Claims Court. This is the cheapest form of legal redress. It can deal with claims for up to £5000 (in England and Wales), although the maximum claim in housing disrepair cases is only £1000. Ask at your local county court (or sheriff's court in Scotland) for details. You do not need a lawyer and the hearings are relatively informal. The court fees range from £20 to £100, depending on the amount of money you are claiming. If you lose your case the most you have to pay is the other side's expenses for attending the hearing. Information is available from Citizens Advice Bureaux and county or sheriff's courts.

Complaining

If you have a complaint about your landlord or the property the first step is to write to your landlord. Keep the tone of the letter pleasant but firm. Clearly state what the problem is and refer to your tenancy agreement to show your landlord that you know your rights. Keep copies of all correspondence. Avoid losing your temper as this will only antagonize the landlord.

If you still have no joy you can pursue your complaint in the following ways:

- If you have rented through an Association of Residential Letting Agents (ARLA) member you may be able to take your case to the association's arbitration service.

- Contact your local Citizens Advice Bureaux for advice. They will help you write letters and will usually negotiate on your behalf.

- If you are seeking compensation – for instance the return of your deposit – you can, as a last resort, take your landlord to court.

£ CASH TIP £

Consider taking out legal expenses insurance. Stand-alone policies can be expensive but you may find that for just £1 a month you can buy this cover as part of your home contents policy or that you get it free as part of your membership of a trade union or professional body. This insurance will usually provide you with a legal helpline which will give you advice and help you write legal letters.

Part 2 Buying

The first few chapters of this section look at the things you need to do before you start house hunting. You should talk to a mortgage lender about the size of home loan you can afford to borrow and how much deposit you will need, and then start to look for a solicitor who will handle the conveyancing.

This is essential in the current property market. Many estate agents will not treat you as a serious buyer unless you already have finance in place. In addition, properties often sell very quickly. If you cannot complete the sale within a few weeks you are at risk of being 'gazumped' – when another buyer offers a higher price and as a result you lose the property and all the fees you have spent on surveyors and conveyancing.

5 Mortgages

Choosing the right mortgage to meet your needs is just as important as picking the right property. But while it may take you months to find the home you want to buy, the chances are that you will put comparatively little thought into selecting a home loan.

It is only when you compare the different interest costs over the life-time of the mortgage that you realize just how much you can save by shopping around for the best mortgage deal.

But with more than 1000 different mortgage products on offer at any one time, it can be very difficult to decide which will offer you the best value. The interest payable on a standard variable-rate mortgage can vary considerably from one mortgage lender to another. It is very much to your advantage, therefore, to spend time comparing what's on offer to ensure that you choose the best-value lender.

First-time buyers account for almost half of all mortgage lending and as such are in a powerful position to negotiate a good rate and shop around. Many lenders offer preferential rates or special offers to first-time buyers, so make the most of these.

When You Should Arrange a Mortgage

In the current fast-moving property market (some homes are selling within days) it is advisable to arrange your mortgage in advance of looking for properties. Often estate agents will want to know you have finance arranged before showing you properties. And if you have a mortgage prearranged you will reduce the risk of being gazumped.

Although you do not need to agree to a particular size of mortgage (this may be difficult as you will not yet know how much you want to borrow), you should arrange the maximum loan that you qualify for 'in principle'. This means that you have applied for the mortgage and the lender has agreed to advance the home loan on certain conditions:

▌ your circumstances do not change

▌ the property is suitable security for the mortgage

▌ you have a sufficient deposit

▌ you meet all the other terms and conditions

Who To Approach for a Mortgage

The days when you had to queue for a mortgage from your local building society are long over. You no longer have the choice of just a bank or building society. Insurance companies, centralized lenders, telephone-based or direct mortgage companies, mortgage advice centres, mortgage brokers and even supermarkets all offer home loans. Surveys have shown that the smaller, local building societies tend to offer cheaper mortgages over the longer term, but they do restrict who they will lend to. Whoever you decide to take a mortgage with, look at that lender's long-term mortgage record to:

▌ ensure that its rates are consistently competitive

▌ check that the lender passes on rate reductions quickly

▌ ensure that the lender is not one of the first to up its mortgage rates when interest rates rise.

Your Bank and/or Building Society

You could approach these first. As you are already a customer and may have saved up a deposit in one of their accounts, they are more likely to consider you for a mortgage.

Another Bank or Building Society

You do not have to have a bank or savings account with a lender to take out a mortgage – although if you don't have one, you will usually be asked to open one if you take out a loan.

A Telephone/Direct Lender

More lenders are offering loans by phone. This means you can get an agreement on a loan very quickly. However, you will not be able to sit down and work through all the figures with the adviser.

A Mortgage Broker/Financial Adviser/Estate Agent

Approaching these first has the advantage of saving you time. If you went to a building society, bank or direct lender you would receive advice only on the mortgage loans offered by that society, bank or direct lender. Mortgage brokers have access to a wide variety of mortgage lenders. Mortgage Brokers can also help those who may otherwise find it hard to get a mortgage. In some cases you may have to pay an arrangement fee – check if you will still have to pay this fee even if you do not go ahead or if the sale falls through.

Regulation of Mortgages

The sale of mortgages is not yet regulated by statute – instead lenders have agreed to abide by a voluntary code of practice. Although a new code of practice was only introduced in the spring of 1997, it has already come under attack.

It means that anyone seeking advice about a mortgage should be aware of the shortfalls of the current consumer protection regime. However, Gordon Brown recently announced that mortgages could be regulated. This is good news for the consumer bodies who have been fighting for change.

The Consumers' Association launched a Campaign for Fair Mortgages in July 1999 after discovering major drawbacks in the way mortgages are sold. It is calling for the Financial Services Authority (FSA) to policy the mortgage industry but until that happens it is a case of buyer beware.

So, until new regulations are introduced, take note that:

▋ the voluntary mortgage code is not being adhered to

▋ bad advice is widespread

▋ many consumers are sold mortgages with an extended lock-in period which ties them in to a variable rate, set entirely at the discretion of the lender

▋ high redemption penalties – some lenders' penalties are not specified at the outset, or are unreasonably high, or both

▋ failure of lenders to pass on mortgage rate cuts in full to consumers – this on a £100,000 mortgage means that consumers are losing out by around £700 per year

▋ failure to be consistent in how lenders treat savers and borrowers – some lenders treat savers and borrowers unfairly when there is a base rate change and make millions of pounds of timing differences (for example, by cutting savings rates a couple of weeks before mortgage rates)

The City watchdogs – and even the police – are investigating the mis-selling of endowment policies.

Despite the bad publicity surrounding these investments (linking a mortgage to a stock market investment is illegal in the United States) and the fact that some will not produce sufficient returns to repay the outstanding mortgage debt at the end of the

25-year term, some three in ten mortgages are still sold on an endowment basis.

This, combined with the fact that the Treasury select committee is investigating the banks and may consider extending statutory regulation to cover mortgages, means that buyers need to think twice about accepting any advice at face value.

Under the existing Mortgage Code lenders must recommend the most suitable product from their range and explain the reasons for recommending a particular mortgage in writing.

This should mean that if an endowment mortgage is not the best type of home loan for you, you should not be pushed into buying one.

However, you should be aware that lenders can opt out of the advice requirement by giving information only.

The code requires that:

▌ you are given full details of mortgage costs, including early redemption penalties

▌ any requirement to buy insurance as part of the mortgage package must be explained

▌ if you are taking out a fixed-rate or discounted mortgage, you will be shown how your repayments are likely to increase at the end of that period (based on the lender's current variable rate)

▌ if the lender is giving you advice it must recommend the most suitable mortgage from its range and state the reasons in writing

▌ lenders must be members of an ombudsman or arbitration scheme to cover complaints

However, if a lender only gives *information* not *advice*, the 'most suitable' rules do not apply. And even if the lender is giving advice, it does not have to ensure that the mortgage is completely suitable, only that it is the most suitable product that is offered by that lender. So if you need a mortgage that is more flexible and the lender does not offer this product, there is no requirement for the lender to tell you so.

How Much Can I Borrow?

This is the first thing you need to know so that you can start looking for properties in your price bracket. Generally you will be required to put down a deposit of at least 5 per cent of the purchase price, although it is possible to take out a 100 per cent home loan which requires no deposit at all.

To get the best deals, you will generally need a much larger deposit of up to 25 per cent of the purchase price. So if you are buying a £50,000 property, you will need a deposit of £12,500.

Generally you can borrow three times your annual salary if you are buying alone. If you are buying with a partner you can borrow up to 2.5 times your joint salary or three times the main salary plus the additional salary.

How much a couple with a joint income of £40,000 can borrow varies from £90,000 to £106,000:

1	Mr A earns £25,000 and Ms B earns £15,000		
	They can either borrow:		
	£75,000 (3 × £25,000) + £15,000	=	£90,000
	or: 2.5 × £40,000 (£25,000 + £15,000)	=	£100,000
2	Mr A earns £33,000 and Ms B earns £7,000		
	They can either borrow:		
	£99,000 (3 × £33,000) + £7,000	=	£106,000
	or: 2.5 × £40,000 (£33,000 + £7,000)	=	£100,000

Generally, if there is not a great difference between each buyer's salary the 2.5 × joint salary option is better. If one buyer earns significantly more, then the 3 × main income + the second salary calculation will qualify the homebuyers for a larger mortgage.

What Earnings Can Be Taken Into Account?

The income you can take into account when working out how much you can borrow is your basic salary before tax and other deductions.

In addition, if part of your earnings are made up of commission or bonuses you may be able to add these to your salary to boost the amount you can borrow. However, your lender will want to see proof that these payments are consistent (if not guaranteed) and will probably require your employer to put this in writing.

If you are self-employed you will generally have to supply three years of audited accounts. The amount you can borrow will usually be based on your average earnings over that three-year period and you will have to supply accounts, tax assessments and often a business plan showing that your future earnings are likely to be the same or greater than in the past. Those who have been self-employed for less than three years should opt for a 'self-certification' mortgage, which requires that you supply details of your income without having to provide proof.

What If You Are New to Your Job?

Most lenders will want to know that your job is secure before advancing a mortgage. Under current employment law you do not have complete job security for the first two years of employment, although the government plans to cut this to one year. As a result you represent a higher lending risk. Your lender may therefore require that you take out mortgage protection insurance to cover your mortgage repayments should you lose your job.

What If You Don't Have a Permanent Employment Contract?

Changing employment patterns mean that an increasing number of workers are no longer given full-time permanent employment. If you work on a contract basis you will probably find it difficult to get a home loan unless you have been consistently employed for the last three years, in which case you may be treated in a similar way to a self-employed borrower.

One option is to opt for a *self-certification mortgage*. These are designed for those who are self-employed and contract workers and borrowers do not require proof of income. Generally the loan must not be more than 75 to 90 per cent of the property's value. However, these loans can come at a price, with interest rates often 0.5 or 1 per cent above the standard variable rate. You will often have to go to a mortgage broker – who will usually charge a fee of 1 per cent of the loan – to arrange this type of mortgage.

Using a Guarantor To Increase the Amount You Can Borrow

If you have a temporary contract, are not in secure employment or do not have enough earnings to borrow the amount you need you can ask a friend or relative (usually your parents) to act as a guarantor.

If you cannot meet the payments they will then become liable. The lender will want to know that the guarantor has sufficient income or equity in their own property to meet your repayments or repay the outstanding loan.

How Much Can You Afford to Borrow?

Even if a lender is prepared to advance you a large mortgage, remember that you must also take into account affordability. Interest rates can rise. In the late 1980s interest rates topped 15 per cent, millions of home buyers struggled to meet their repayments and tens of thousands had their homes repossessed. Check you would still be able to afford your mortgage if interest rates rose to double figures once again (see Appendix).

The alternative is to opt for a fixed or capped rate mortgage (these are explained later in this chapter), which will limit the maximum interest rate you will have to pay.

Lenders will often look at all your outgoings before deciding whether or not you can afford your mortgage repayments. Generally your monthly repayments should not exceed one third of your take-home pay. That way, if mortgage rates rise you will still be able to afford your repayments.

Your lender may ask you to fill in a questionnaire asking what your other outgoings are each month to make sure that you can afford to meet your monthly mortgage payments. You can work this out for yourself. Add up your monthly outgoings (if you don't have final figures use rough approximations):

▊ monthly mortgage repayments plus life insurance/endowment premiums

▊ service charges and ground rent (if you are buying a leasehold property)

- insurance

- interest on other loans and credit cards

- gas/electricity/telephone bill

- travel/motoring costs

- food, clothes, entertainment

- and any other commitments, such as maintenance payments

then deduct this from your monthly after-tax income. You should find that you can easily afford to meet all these costs. Be realistic when estimating your outgoings and remember that once you buy a property it tends to be a drain on your finances. You will have to pay for furniture, renovations, repairs, maintenance and decoration.

Affordability varies in line with house prices and mortgage rates. At the height of the property market boom, the average buyer paid more than a quarter of their income in mortgage costs. That is now down to around 15 per cent

Helping to Finance Your Mortgage

For many first-time buyers paying monthly mortgage repayments is a struggle. Although you may qualify for a certain size of home loan and meet the affordability criteria, once you move into your property you will find that the extra costs can soar. But there are ways to help you meet these.

Cash Backs

A few lenders offer 'cash backs', usually amounting to a few hundred pounds as an incentive for borrowers to take out a particular mortgage. These are explained in the section covering different types of mortgages. These cash backs can help you through those first few expensive months when you move into a property.

Renting Out a Room

If you tell your lender that you intend to finance your mortgage by taking in a lodger or renting out part of the property, the lender is likely to think twice about advancing you such a large home loan. However, there is nothing to stop you taking in a lodger and under the Rent-A-Room scheme this rent can be *tax free.*

Most mortgage contracts require that borrowers seek permission from the lender before renting out a property. This is to ensure that you don't end up with a sitting tenant, as this will affect the value and saleability of the property. However, lodgers are usually exempt from this requirement. This is because they have no security of tenure (no rights).

In the current tax year you can earn £4250 a year in rent tax free provided:

▌ you rent out only one room in your property

▌ that room is furnished

▌ you don't rent out the room as a business (you are not running a B&B or guest house)

If you earn more than this allowance you can either:

▌ earn the first £4250 a year tax free and then pay tax on the amount of rent over this limit (at your top rate of tax); or

▌ pay tax on your profits – rent minus expenses

Generally if your expenses are less than £4250 a year you will be better off claiming the Rent-A-Room allowance. Expenses can include a proportion of: the mortgage, insurance, gas, electricity and cleaning. If you have four rooms in your home and rent out one, you can generally claim a quarter of these costs. In addition you can deduct as an expense roughly 10 per cent of the rent to cover wear and tear of furnishings and the costs of advertising for a lodger.

Another alternative is to buy a property but not move into it for the first year. Rental incomes are currently running at between 6 and 10 per cent, so you should find that the rental covers the entire mortgage and earns you a small profit. At the same time you can hope to make a capital appreciation on the property. When your finances are less stretched you can then move into the property. Remember, you will have to earn enough in rent to cover the mortgage easily, you must ensure that the property is let with the agreement of your lender on a shorthold tenancy and you must be prepared to have weeks or months when you do not have a tenant/ are advertising for a new tenant and will have to pay your mortgage and for renting alternative accommodation elsewhere.

How Much Can You Borrow Against the Value of a Property?

In addition to the size of mortgage a lender will advance as a multiple of your salary, the loan to value ratio will also affect the amount you can borrow. The ratio is the size of the mortgage in relation to the value of the property.

Generally, you will be required to pay at least a 5 per cent deposit. Although some lenders do offer 100 per cent home loans these are usually more expensive – interest rates can be higher and you will have to pay a high borrowing premium (see mortgage indemnity insurance).

To qualify for the cheapest home loans, you generally need to have a deposit of around 25 per cent.

Mortgage Indemnity

This is an extra cost that many homebuyers forget to budget for. It is an insurance charge that is paid by the borrower to protect the lender against losses should the buyer fall into arrears. Remember, although you as the buyer must pay the premium it protects the lender – not you. And if you are repossessed and the home is sold for less than the outstanding debt you could still be pursued for the losses, even though you have paid for the lender to have insurance against these losses.

The premium must generally be paid by those taking out a home loan for more than 75 to 90 per cent of the property value. Most major lenders, like the Halifax, now require a much higher loan to value ratio – in other words a smaller deposit – before charging mortgage indemnity. The standard is now 90 per cent. Mortgage indemnity is charged on a sliding scale and can rise to 10 per cent of the outstanding loan on a 100 per cent mortgage. But it is only paid on the proportion above 75 per cent (in a few cases this can vary).

So if you are buying a £100,000 property with no deposit the costs could be as much as 10 per cent of £25,000 (25 per cent of the mortgage) or £2500. For 85 per cent mortgages the rate falls to about 7 per cent. But rates charged do vary.

On a £60,000 mortgage you can pay between £500 and £1400 in mortgage indemnity insurance if you have only a 5 per cent deposit.

To help borrowers meet the costs, lenders often allow the premium to be added to the outstanding mortgage loan. The snag with this is that the borrower will end up paying interest on it for 25 years. So if you can find an alternative way to finance it do your sums and you may find that over the longer run it is cheaper to pay for it in cash or to fund it using a low-rate shorter-term loan.

Some lenders allow homebuyers to pay the mortgage indemnity in 36 monthly instalments at the start of the loan. These extra payments should be taken into account when budgeting.

Warning: Not all lenders call their extra charge mortgage indemnity insurance. Some call it a high lending fee and others a scheme for maximum advances. So you may not realize what you are paying for or the fact that it provides you with no protection at all.

£ CASH TIP £

A few lenders no longer charge mortgage indemnity insurance. But this should not influence your mortgage choice entirely – weigh up the overall costs.

£ CASH TIP £

You cannot shop around for the best mortgage indemnity deal as you must purchase the one arranged by your lender. But you should compare the premiums charged by different lenders as premiums do vary.

£ CASH TIP £

The larger the deposit, the cheaper the mortgage indemnity. Some lenders will still charge mortgage indemnity insurance if you have a deposit of 25 per cent or less. Find out what rates are charged on different sizes of loan. By putting down a slightly larger deposit you may be able to save hundreds of pounds.

For instance, if you are buying a £50,000 property with a £2500 deposit and mortgage indemnity is charged at 7.25 per cent on loans greater than 75 per cent of loan-to-value you would pay:

£47,500 (£50,000 purchase price – £2500 deposit) –
£37,500 (75% of the loan to value) = £10,000
7.25% mortgage indemnity × £10,000 = £725

If you put down a further £100 deposit to bring the loan to value down to under 95 per cent and the mortgage indemnity rate fell to 6 per cent you would pay:

£47,400 (£50,000 – £2600 deposit) – £37,500 (75% of
loan to value) = £9,900
6% mortgage indemnity × £9,900 = £594

So an additional £100 deposit will save you £131 in mortgage indemnity premiums. Although few cases will be this clear-cut, this gives an example of the savings that could be made.

> **Warning:** Most insurers have agreed with lenders that they can pursue the borrower for any shortfall – if the property is repossessed and sold for less than the amount of the outstanding mortgage and arrears. Some lenders have now stated that they will not chase evicted homebuyers for these debts. But it can still happen, even if the lender can recoup all or most of the losses from the mortgage indemnity insurance. So even after you have been repossessed and your property sold on – often for a fraction of the price you could have obtained – you may still be liable for the outstanding debt.

What If I Don't Have a Deposit?

As already discussed, you will generally need a 5 per cent deposit. So if you are buying a £50,000 property, you will need to have £2500 as a deposit. Remember that in addition to this deposit you will also have to fund legal/conveyancing costs, stamp duty, removal costs, insurance and possibly a mortgage arrangement fee.

However, if – once you have budgeted for these extras – you find that you do not have a sufficient deposit there are ways to get round this problem:

▌ 100 per cent home loans – a few lenders offer these, as do some housebuilders. You may have to pay a higher interest rate and your mortgage indemnity premiums will be high. Banks who currently offer 100 per cent loans include Bank of Scotland, Royal Bank of Scotland, Sainsbury's Bank and Scottish Widows.

▌ Borrowing the deposit – your lender will probably not be impressed if you say that you are borrowing the deposit. However, if you can persuade your parents to lend you the cash on an informal basis this will get round this problem. If you take out a mortgage with a *cash back* you may be able to repay all or part of the loan almost immediately.

Buying with a Friend/Your Partner

In some cases the only way you can afford to get on to the property ladder is to buy the property with your partner, spouse, a relative or a friend.

The advantage is that you can borrow more money – usually three times the main salary plus the other salary or two-and-a-half times the joint income – and can split the costs.

The disadvantages are that if you fall out or if one of you wishes to sell and the other does not want to move, you could find that one buyer cannot afford to buy out the other owner. You may then be forced to sell the property even if you don't want to move. Also if the joint-purchaser fails to meet his or her monthly mortgage repayments you will be jointly liable for the debts.

The risks of things going wrong are high, particularly if you do not have a long-term commitment to your relationship or friendship. Even married couples face a high risk, with one in three marriages ending in divorce.

A straightforward repayment loan may be better than an endowment mortgage in these cases as you will not be forced to sell your endowment (which will mean you suffer early surrender penalties) and it is easier to work out how much has been paid and how much is owing. The alternative is to take out separate endowment policies. However, if one party dies the endowment will only cover half of the loan so an additional term assurance policy may be necessary. Some insurers offer twin-plan endowment schemes which give separate endowment policies but joint life cover.

Types of Joint Ownership

If you are buying a property with another person you have two choices:

▌ joint tenancy, or

▌ tenancy in common

Joint tenancies are the most common. Each person is assumed to own half the equity and if one partner dies the other inherits that person's share of the property, irrespective of what their will says.

Tenancy in common, the legal alternative, allows for varying financial arrangements. If you draw up a trust deed you can set down exactly how much each person has invested in the home. So if one partner has paid a bigger share of the deposit or pays more towards the mortgage the deed enables the buyers to agree at the outset what will happen to the property should the relationship break down. Tenancy in common allows each of the owners to leave their share of the property in their will as they wish.

What If I Can't Find an Affordable Property?

Shared Ownership

For those who cannot afford to buy a home but who still want to get on to the property ladder, shared ownership is an option. Under these schemes you part rent and part buy. Most of these schemes are run by housing associations.

In London, the London Home Ownership Group is an umbrella body of 30 associations which offer 5000 homes a year to those who cannot afford to buy outright. Buyers do not have to be housing association or council tenants. Prices start from £15,000 of the available share and the typical age group for applicants is between 25 and 35 years old. However, people of any age can apply and no preference is given to younger people.

These schemes can help those who cannot save up the 10 per cent deposit usually required. The homebuyer buys a minimum of 25 per cent of the property with a mortgage and pays rent on the remainder. As his or her income rises or more capital is raised, further tranches of equity can be bought until the buyer owns 100 per cent of the property. These extra 'shares' of the property are then revalued by an independent surveyor.

> **Warning:** Buyers can usually buy the remaining shares in the property in a maximum of four tranches. But as the price depends on the market value these extra tranches can cost far more than the first. So buyers may find that as prices continue to rise, they can never afford to buy the whole of the property.

The rent will not normally include insurance, repairs and maintenance. If you buy and rent with a 50/50 split the costs usually work out 30 per cent cheaper than buying outright.

Some lenders are reluctant to lend on this basis because the homebuyer does not own the entire property and therefore there is less security. However, some associations do underwrite any mortgage arrears.

Often the association has the right to find a suitable buyer at market value should the tenant want to sell. If no buyer is found within three months, then the owner has the right to sell the property on the open market.

Contacts: Metropolitan Home Ownership (020 8881 1234); The Housing Corporation (020 7393 2000).

Part Ownership

Some developers offer homebuyers the option of buying 75 per cent of the property now and the remaining 25 per cent at a later date.

The advantage is that initially you only have to pay three-quarters of the mortgage you would have paid on a comparable property.

However, after five years (this is the usual term) when you have to pay for the additional 25 per cent of the property you could find that you cannot afford it. Developers usually make you pay the market price and if the property market has boomed you could find that the 25 per cent share costs almost double what it would have originally cost. However, if the market has done well you should be able to sell the property reasonably easily and repay the remaining 25 per cent share out of the proceeds of the sale.

The Mortgage Application

What Information You Will Need To Supply

You will need to provide:

- proof of income

- details of other spending commitments such as outstanding loans

- bank details

- details of your current landlord (possibly)/amount of rent you are paying

- details of your employment record

The lender will then want to check with your employer that you:

- are employed on a permanent contract (and since when)

- earn the salary/overtime/bonuses that you claim

You may be required to arrange life insurance/an endowment policy at the same time as taking out your mortgage. For this you will need to fill in a questionnaire asking for details about your current and past state of health and any medical conditions. You may need to undergo a medical examination.

What Information the Lender Will Check

Before advancing a loan, the lender will want to know that you are creditworthy. It will probably write to your employer/landlord/bank and check with a credit reference agency to find out:

▌ if you have any county court judgements against you for non-payment of debts

▌ if you have other outstanding loans/credit

▌ your payment history – if you manage your finances well or have run into difficulty with loan/credit repayments in the past

Choosing a Mortgage

There are several things you must consider. The extra costs of taking out a mortgage are often overlooked. The actual cost of taking out a home loan can vary widely, even though on the surface there seems to be no difference in mortgage rates or terms. This is because interest can be charged in different ways, mortgage indemnity premiums vary and you may have to purchase extra products (mortgage repayment protection insurance or buildings and contents insurance). Another hidden 'cost' is that investment performance on endowment policies varies widely and as such one home loan could leave you far better off than another. So the golden rule is: do not just compare interest rates – look at the total costs and benefits of a mortgage.

Different Types of Mortgage

Repayment Mortgages

Each month you pay interest on the amount outstanding and repay an element of your outstanding debt.

Pros:
▌ Safe – if you make all the payments your loan will be repaid at the end of the mortgage term.

▌ If you switch mortgages you don't have to worry about taking out an extra endowment policy to cover a larger mortgage. Although you may have to take out life cover to pay the extra loan.

▌ They are much easier to understand and select. With interest-only mortgages you have to compare interest costs and select the best performing repayment vehicle. With repayments you need only pick the best rate.

Cons:
▌ At the end of the mortgage you have no lump sum. Endowment mortgages aim to repay the loan and may produce an extra cash payment.

Don't forget to add in the costs of separate life assurance (term assurance) that should be taken out to pay off your loan if you die.

Interest-only Mortgages

With these the homebuyer only pays interest on the outstanding loan and then contributes to an investment which should produce sufficient returns to pay off the loan at the end of the mortgage term. None of the outstanding debt is repaid until the end of the term or when you sell your property. The most popular interest-only mortgages are backed by endowments, but they can also be linked to personal pensions and Individual Savings Accounts (ISAs).

Pros:
▌ If your investment performs well you may have more than enough to repay your outstanding mortgage and have an extra tax-free lump sum on top.

▌ With good investment performance (and a flexible repayment investment) you could repay your loan early.

▌ Endowments (and usually pension plans) have life insurance built in so you do not have to pay for extra life cover.

Cons:
▌ You do not repay any of the outstanding debt, so if you want to sell your property you will still have to repay the same size mortgage that you borrowed at the outset.

▌ The value of your investment/endowment may not be sufficient to repay your mortgage at the end of the term. If investment performance is poor you may have to increase your premiums to cover any potential shortfall.

Endowment Mortgages

If you decide that you want an endowment mortgage, you must then select the type of endowment policy that will best suit your needs. In some cases you will not be given a choice and must take out the endowment policy that the lender sells (most are tied to or own life insurance companies).

In recent years there have been warnings that some endowments will not produce sufficient investment returns to meet the outstanding loan at the end of the mortgage. However, this problem has mainly been concentrated among those with short-term mortgages.

In most cases endowments need a growth of 8 to 10 per cent a year to pay off the debt. At the moment most 10-year policies are giving returns of around 10 per cent and 25-year plans around 13 per cent. However, performance does vary.

So, in addition to picking a mortgage with a competitive mortgage rate you must also pick one with a good performing endowment policy.

Warning: If you need to cash in your endowment policy early or get into financial difficulties and can no longer afford the premiums you could get only a fraction of your investment returned. Once you have taken out an endowment policy you must keep paying the premiums for the full 25 years to get the maximum returns.

Different types of endowment policies

With profits: With these you share in the profits of the life fund with bonuses added annually. Once added to your fund these bonuses cannot be taken away, even if the stock market crashes. At the end of the policy term you receive a terminal or final bonus.

Unit linked: With these your premiums buy units in a life fund and the value of these can rise or fall depending on the underlying performance of the fund. As a result, the value of your fund can drop if the stock market falls. In the last few years of the policy your investments are switched to safer funds to prevent a stock market crash wiping out some of your final pay-out. You may be given a choice of funds but will generally be advised to invest in a safe managed fund.

Unitized with profits: These are slightly newer types of endowment policy and combine features of both the others. You buy units in a fund but receive annual bonuses.

Performance of endowment policies

As discussed above, it is essential to pick a good performing endowment policy as well as a low mortgage rate – and in some cases a top performing endowment can earn you far more than any savings you could make by taking out a cheaper home loan.

A man who took out a with-profits endowment 25 years ago (when he was aged 29) and paid in £20 a month would have received around £40,000 on average from his endowment policy at the end of the term. But according to a survey by *Money Marketing* magazine the difference between the top performing fund (which paid out £49,257) and the poorest performer (which paid out £29,742) was almost £20,000. If you took out a £60,000 mortgage which cost you an average of 8 per cent interest, but could have taken out a mortgage that cost an average of 7.5 per cent, you would pay some £7000 in extra interest over the term of the mortgage. This extra interest will cost you nowhere near as much as the losses you could suffer by picking a poor performing endowment policy.

In recent years there have been warnings that some endowments will not produce enough investment returns to meet the outstanding loan at the end of the mortgage. Yet most homebuyers with endowments expect that they will not only repay the loan, but that it will pay them an additional lump sum on top. This problem has mainly been concentrated among those with short-term mortgages.

In most cases endowments need a growth of 8 to 10 per cent a year to pay off the debt. However, when inflation falls so do investment returns. However, even at the moment most 10-year policies are giving returns of around 9 to 10 per cent and 25-year plans around 13 per cent. If yours is a short-term endowment or a poor performing one, your insurance company or lender may ask you to increase contributions. Alternatively, if you receive a lump sum such as a large annual bonus you can repay some of the loan, but check that there are no penalties for doing so.

ISA Mortgages

These use Individual Savings Accounts as the investment vehicle to repay your mortgage. The advantages are that they are tax-free investments and much more flexible than endowments, so that if the fund performs well you can decrease or stop your payments or repay your mortgage early. The drawback of ISAs is that they are directly linked to the stock market and as such their value can rise as well as fall. Life insurance must be arranged separately.

Pension Mortgages

Remember your pension is primarily there to provide an income for retirement. Although there are currently tax breaks on pensions which means you receive tax relief at your highest rate on contributions and a tax-free lump sum on retirement, these tax breaks may not be guaranteed by future governments. You usually need to arrange separate life insurance, although you can receive tax relief on some life insurance contributions if they are part of your personal pension.

Pros:
▌ Significant tax advantages.

Cons:
▌ You may have less money on which to retire and you will have used up this valuable tax break on a mortgage rather than your pension.

Flexible Mortgages

These are relatively new types of home loan. You do not have to pay a fixed amount each month for the life of the mortgage and can increase, decrease or temporarily stop payments to suit your circumstances. These loans appeal to the self-employed, those with variable earnings and those who expect to earn large bonuses which they want to use to pay off chunks of their mortgage.

Some flexible mortgages are linked to current accounts and work as a combined loan and current account. Flexible mortgages can also offer repayment breaks of up to six months. However, the rates may not be the lowest on the market.

Pros:
▌ You can overpay each month to reduce the size of your loan.

▌ You can also use bonuses or windfalls to reduce your mortgage.

▌ If you have a change of circumstances – for instance if you start a family – you can reduce payments and underpay (often for six months).

▌ Some lenders also allow repayment holidays.

▌ If you have paid off some of your mortgage you can then take a lump sum out of your mortgage account to fund another purchase.

Cons:
▌ You will not qualify for the cheapest mortgage deals or cash back offers, but some lenders do offer incentive payments (of up to 3 per cent of the mortgage advance).

▌ In some cases the minimum overpayment must be £500 or £2000, so you may not be able to overpay small amounts each month.

The popularity of flexible mortgages is growing because the advantages are so great. At time of print 29 lenders offer flexible mortgages. The great thing is that you can pay off your mortgage early by as much as 10 or 15 years and save thousands of pounds.

There are no penalties for paying off your mortgage quickly and no charges for overpayment. You can also take payment holidays when money is tight. Add to this the fact that interest is calculated daily rather than annually and the savings add up to thousands of pounds over your mortgage term. For example, a customer with a £210,000 flexible mortgage with the Abbey National saves £17,000 over a 15-year term when compared with a fixed standard variable rate mortgage.

Paying your mortgage off early is a particularly good idea in times of low inflation when your outstanding debt does not decrease due to rising inflation. By paying in as little as £5 a week extra you can cut your mortgage term and save thousands.

Table 5.1 How much does it cost to pay flexible mortgages off quickly?

Size of mortgage	Reduction in term	Saving in interest
Pay in £5 extra a week		
£40,000	4 years 9 months	£10,551.64
£80,000	3 years 1 month	£14,581.61
£120,000	2 years 5 months	£18,124.10
Pay in £10 extra a week		
£40,000	7 years 5 months	£15,478.66
£80,000	4 years 9 months	£21,103.38
£120,000	3 years 8 months	£25,373.43
Pay in £20 extra a week		
£40,000	10 years 11 months	£21,788.22
£80,000	7 years 5 months	£30,957.38
£120,000	5 years 9 months	£37,186.56

All figures based on an interest rate of 6.7 per cent
Source: Yorkshire Bank

Variable, Fixed, Capped or Discount?

Discounted and fixed rate mortgages account for some 40 per cent of new home loans, so are less popular than in 1998, when they accounted for 60 per cent of new loans. However, because lenders can show the initial APR (the annual percentage rate of interest which reflects the true cost of borrowing) these can be difficult to compare. Always look at the cost of borrowing over the full term of the mortgage. And watch out for redemption penalties if you switch or cash in your mortgage, as in some cases you will have to pay a financial penalty of six months' or more interest.

Variable Rate Mortgages

The rate of most standard mortgages varies in line with interest rate moves. So you gain if rates fall, but must bear the brunt of any interest rate rises. See annually adjusted mortgages below.

Pros:
▌ More flexible, as you can usually cash in your mortgage without financial penalties.

Cons:
▌ If rates rise significantly you could find it difficult to meet your monthly mortgage payments.

Warning: Some lenders take longer than others to pass on interest rate reductions and some increase rates more quickly when they rise. Over the term of a mortgage, the timing of rate moves can add considerably to the cost of your mortgage.

Tracker Mortgages

Tracker mortgages guarantee that your mortgage rate will track the Bank of England base rate. So any cuts in interest rates will be passed on to you as the borrower. This should be the case with standard variable rate mortgages; however, lenders are not always very good at passing on full base rate cuts – to their credit, lenders don't always hike their rates to the full amount when interest rates rise either.

Annually Adjusted Mortgages

One third of all mortgages have the monthly repayments adjusted annually – not when interest rates change. Although the amount of interest you are charged will change when interest rates rise and fall, your actual repayments do not. At the end of the year (usually in the spring) your monthly repayments will be adjusted to reflect any under- or overpayment of interest. When interest rates rise you may find that you are paying far less for your home loan than those with standard variable mortgages. However, when rates fall you are likely to pay more. Over the life-time of your mortgage you should not pay any more or less than with another type of home loan.

Pros:
▌ You know at the beginning of the year how much your monthly repayments will be.

Cons:
▌ If interest rates have risen significantly you could face a large increase in your monthly repayments once the annual adjustment takes place.

Fixed Rate Mortgages

Fixed rate mortgages are usually a safe option when interest rates are set to rise. However, you will find that rates are higher than for variable mortgages if lenders believe rate rises are likely.

The fixed rate usually applies for the first one to five years.

Pros:
▌ You know how much you will have to pay for the term of the fixed rate and if rates rise you will pay less than those with variable mortgages.

Cons:
▌ If rates are lower over the term of your fixed rate you will pay more interest than with a variable loan.

▋ When the fixed rate ends you can find that your monthly mortgage payments jump significantly.

▋ These loans are less flexible and if you cash in your mortgage in the first few years you could have to pay several months' interest as a penalty.

Warning: Once the fixed rate period has finished you may be obliged to remain with the lender for a number of years or pay a financial penalty. So if the lender charges a higher-than-average rate you could lose out.

£ CASH TIP £

Do not take out a fixed rate mortgage if you expect that interest rates will fall to below the level of the fix during the fixed rate period.

£ CASH TIP £

Check that the loan is portable so that you can take it with you if you are moving up the property ladder. If it is not, and you need to cash in your mortgage you will usually face financial penalties.

Warning: If you fall into arrears with a fixed rate loan the penalties can be much higher than with other mortgages. So ask before taking out the mortgage.

Capped Rate Mortgages

These are less common, but will appeal at a time of rising mortgage rates as they guarantee that rates will not rise above a set level or cap. In some cases they are 'collared', which means that a minimum rate of interest has also been set so any rate reductions below this level will not be passed on to the borrower. These are known as cap and collar mortgages. The capped rate can apply for anything from the first five years to the full term of the mortgage.

Pros:
▋ You know that for the period of the capped rate you will never pay more than a certain level of interest.

Cons:
▋ If you cash in your mortgage in the first few years you may have to pay financial penalties.

▋ If the mortgage also has a minimum interest rate you could find that if interest rates fall you will not get the benefit of very low mortgage rates.

Discount Mortgages

These give you a discount of anything between 0.25 and 5 per cent off the variable rate of interest for the first few months or years of the mortgage. These are only usually offered to

▋ first-time buyers

▋ new borrowers (who are switching their mortgage from another lender)

Pros:
▋ For the term of the discount you will pay less than other borrowers.

Cons:

▮ Check what rate will apply after the discount period has ended as you may have to pay a higher rate than other borrowers.

▮ There are usually high penalties for all or part repayment of the loan in the first few years and borrowers may be required to repay all of the discount if they cash in their mortgage.

£ CASH TIP £

Check that the interest is discounted and not deferred. If it is deferred it will be added to the outstanding loan and you could end up with a larger mortgage than you started with.

Incentives

Tough competition between mortgage lenders means that many offer first-time and new borrowers inducements.

At time of print many mortgage companies are offering appealing incentives. For example, Alliance & Leicester offers first-time buyers no mortgage indemnity (MIP) for advances up to 90 per cent on their 6.85 per cent variable rate mortgage. Bank of Scotland Mortgages Direct offers free accident, sickness and unemployment insurance for six months and no MIP for advances up to 90 per cent on their variable rate mortgage at 5.99 per cent. The Halifax's variable rate mortgage at 6.85 per cent offers all borrowers no MIP and free valuation fees via a nominated solicitor. Cash incentives whereby they refund a set percentage of the loan on completion are no longer so common.

Free Services

Some lenders offer to waive the valuation fee or pay for some of your legal costs.

The Mortgage Term

Although most mortgages are taken over a 25-year period or term there is nothing to stop you choosing a shorter or longer pay back term from 10 to 30 years.

With a repayment mortgage, the shorter the term the higher the monthly costs.

With an interest-only loan, the length of the mortgage term makes no difference to the interest payments since the debt stays the same. However, you will have to invest more in either your endowment, PEP or pension plan to ensure that your investment is adequately funded to repay the loan at the end of a shorter mortgage term. So if you want a shorter-term mortgage, a repayment mortgage may be the better option.

If you cut a £80,000 mortgage term from 25 years to 15 years and pay an interest rate of 6.85 per cent you will pay £72,500 less interest over the term of the mortgage for an extra monthly repayment of less than £200. The only problem is that if you are borrowing near the maximum allowed and rates increase you will probably find it hard to meet your monthly mortgage bill. However, as you will be repaying the capital much faster, if you have to move you will have greater equity in the property. Table 2 illustrates the effect of reducing the mortgage term on monthly repayments.

Table 5.2: How reducing the mortgage term increases monthly repayments

Term of loan	Monthly cost	
	£55,000 loan	*£75,000 loan*
10 years	£630.93	£866.58
15 years	£481.35	£662.61
20 years	£410.49	£565.98
25 years	£370.88	£511.97

All figures assume no MIRAS on a repayment mortgage at 6.85 per cent
Source: Halifax.

Comparing the Cost of Different Mortgages

Mortgages are no longer straightforward. Cash backs, discounts, fixed rates and arrangement fees mean you will have to compare more than just the interest rates. These are the aspects of the mortgage you should compare:

Endowment v repayment: Don't just compare the monthly payments. With a repayment mortgage you should add any life insurance premiums to the monthly costs and with an interest-only mortgage the endowment premiums or the costs of another type of repayment investment.

Interest rates and how interest is charged: Mortgages have been covered by 'annual percentage rate' rules since 1987. The APR should give the true cost of borrowing and include the cost of any mortgage indemnity guarantee, brokerage or arrangement fees, valuation costs, redemption penalties and compulsory insurances. However, because the APR can be given on the initial fixed or discount rate it makes the true cost over 25 years very difficult to compare.

The best way to compare costs is to add up 12-monthly repayments over 25 years. Take into account any discounts or short-term fixed rates.

Also you will find that interest is charged in different ways. Most building societies take payments in advance, but bank mortgages are usually paid in arrears.

Homebuyers with *repayment mortgages* could be paying £73 billion in unnecessary interest charges on their mortgages over the next 25 years because not all lenders calculate interest in the same way, according to calculations from Yorkshire Bank.

Most lenders calculate interest annually, basing the next 12 months' payments on the mortgage balance outstanding on the first day of the year. No account is made of payments credited to the repayment mortgage over the subsequent 12-month period. This costs borrowers some £160 million a year.

The other way that homebuyers lose is that only a few lenders calculate interest daily, working out interest on the balance outstanding at the end of each day. The total interest on a £51,000 repayment mortgage over 25 years, assuming an interest rate of 7.24 per cent, would be £60,783 if calculated on an annual basis. Calculated on a daily basis, the total interest would be only £47,103.

Redemption penalties: If you agree to pay redemption penalties (a charge if you cash your mortgage in within the first few years) you will usually be offered a lower mortgage rate. However, if you do need to move you could find that the savings of a fixed rate or discount mortgage do not make up for the redemption costs.

> **Warning:** Think twice before making additional mortgage payments as some loans do not allow even part repayments of the mortgage without triggering redemption penalties.

£ CASH TIP £

In many cases lenders allow you to take your mortgage with you when you move. This way you avoid hefty redemption penalties – often totalling up to several thousand pounds.

Arrangement fees: In some cases you may be charged an arrangement fee. Always ask in advance what this will be, and if it will be refunded should you be forced to pull out of a property purchase.

Tied products: In some cases you may be required to take out buildings and contents insurance arranged by the lender as a condition of the loan. If the insurance is much more expensive than you can arrange elsewhere you will lose out.

How to Calculate the Costs of Different Mortgages

You should add up how much the mortgage will cost you in total – not just the monthly repayments. It is usually advisable to compare the costs over the entire term of a mortgage. But as first-time buyers usually move up the property ladder after a few years, compare the costs in the first five years.

For instance, if the prevailing variable mortgage rate is 8 per cent and there are several different types of mortgage on offer, these are how the costs could compare on a £50,000 interest-only mortgage:

- Mortgage A: standard variable rate: £303.34 a month.
  Five-year cost: £18,200.40.

- Mortgage B: fixed rate of 7 per cent for three years, a £250 arrangement fee, then the standard variable rate, compulsory insurance that works out at £100 a year more expensive than the best deal.
  Five-year cost: £17,477.28.

- Mortgage C: 2 per cent discount for two years, no arrangement fees.
  Five-year cost: £16,380.24.

- Mortgage D: 5 per cent cash back but buyer then has to pay 0.5 per cent above the market rate.
  Five-year cost: £16,838.

Mortgage Illustrations

When you approach a bank, building society, financial adviser or mortgage broker to discuss a mortgage you should be given a mortgage illustration. This will usually show:

- the amount of the loan (and the value of the property)

- the term of the loan (number of years)

- the number of monthly repayments

- the interest rate

- the gross monthly mortgage payments

- the net payments (after tax relief)

▌ the total gross amount payable over the term of the loan (and what this includes – life insurance/endowment premiums are usually in addition)

▌ the APR and what this includes such as
  – legal fees
  – valuation fees
  – any arrangement/administration fees
  – mortgage guarantee insurance/indemnity insurance fees
  – remittance fees and any other costs

▌ the amount and cost of term assurance to protect a repayment loan, or the endowment if you are taking out an endowment mortgage

▌ the warnings 'YOUR HOME IS AT RISK IF YOU DO NOT KEEP UP REPAYMENTS ON A MORTGAGE OR OTHER LOANS SECURED ON IT' and 'Be sure you can afford the repayments before entering into a credit agreement'

▌ details of any other products you have to buy as a condition of the loan (for instance buildings insurance).

You should also be given an illustration of the costs of any insurance you take out to protect your mortgage repayments should you lose your job or become too ill to work. *Do not confuse mortgage protection plans for payment protection plans. The former is often used to describe term life assurance policies and does not protect repayments, only the outstanding loan in the event of death.*

Read the illustration carefully. If, for instance, there are extra fees – such as arrangement fees – included on the illustration, but you were not told earlier that you would have to pay them, do not assume they are listed in error.

The Agreement in Principle/Mortgage Certificate

If the lender agrees a loan it will often give you a certificate showing how much it is prepared to lend (subject to a valuation and structural survey of the property). It will state that this offer is only valid for a limited period. Often this is as little as six weeks, but it can be for up to three months.

As it may take you weeks or even months to find a property to suit your needs you may want to keep your mortgage options open.

If you have secured a particularly good deal on a mortgage you may be able to agree with the lender that the mortgage you want is held for a specific period of time. In this case you will have to sign a form accepting the mortgage offer. Then, once your offer on a particular property has been accepted, you can finalize the mortgage advance.

Protecting Your Mortgage Repayments

Some 2.5 million of the 10 million homebuyers risk serious arrears on their mortgage payments if they become sick or unemployed. Cuts in social security mean it is now advisable to buy insurance that will cover your monthly repayments. Eighty per cent of borrowers receive no assistance with mortgage interest payments for the first nine months after stopping work.

It is usually easier and cheaper to take out this cover at the same time as your mortgage. You do not have to buy it from your mortgage lender but can shop around to find a lender that offers this insurance at a cheaper rate.

Lenders are now offering more than just mortgage protection insurance. Some offer a mix of life insurance, critical illness cover (which pays a lump sum if you suffer a specific medical condition such as a heart attack), permanent health insurance (which pays you an income for a set period of time if you can no longer work due to ill health or redundancy) and unemployment cover in one policy.

Since 1 July 1999, new standards in mortgage payment protection insurance (MPPI) have been in place. All policies must pay out after a maximum of 60 days – in the past policies have had excess periods of up to 120 days. But still watch out for the small print, check for exclusions and find out for how long payments will be made.

> **Warning:** Read the small print of your mortgage protection policy, especially if you are self-employed or a contract worker. If you are made redundant, you may not receive the full 12-month pay out if your contract would have finished before the end of the 12 months.

Mortgage Tax Relief

Mortgage interest tax relief (MIRAS) is given on the first £30,000 of your loan. The current rate of tax relief is 10 per cent. This will be abolished from April 2000.

Table 5.3: How the abolition of MIRAS will affect monthly mortgage bills

Size of loan	Tax relief 10%	No tax relief
Repayment		
£35,000	£229.79	£246.91
£55,000	£370.88	£388.00
£75,000	£511.97	£529.09
£100,000	£688.34	£705.45
Endowment		
£35,000	£199.80	£182.67
£55,000	£313.96	£296.84
£75,000	£428.13	£411.00
£100,000	£553.71	£570.84

Assuming a 25-year term and an interest rate of 6.85 per cent.
Source: Halifax

6 Preliminaries: Costs Appraisal and Appointing a Solicitor/Conveyancer

Budgeting for the Extra Costs

If you are buying a house costing £50,000 you will need to find nearly £800 in solicitors, and search fees. This figure goes up to nearly £2000 on a £100,000 property and over £3000 on a £200,000 property.

Be prepared for a potential purchase to fall through. Often you may have to pay for more than one survey and extra legal fees. Table 4 illustrates the typical costs of buying a home. Two companies now offer cheap anti-gazumping insurance that will reimburse you on things like legal and valuation fees. Legal & General and Lambeth Building Society charge between £15 and £30 for their policies.

Stamp Duty

This is a tax that has to be paid on property costing over £60,000 and is charged at 1 per cent of the total purchase price (not just the proportion above £60,000). It rises to 1.5 per cent on properties over £250,000 and 3.5 per cent above £500,000. So if you buy a property that is worth less than £60,000 you pay no stamp duty. But on a property worth £100,000 you will pay £1000.

£ CASH TIP £

If you are buying a property valued just above one of these stamp duty bands you can agree a purchase price below the band level and make up the difference by agreeing a separate figure for curtains, carpets and other fixtures and fittings.

Legal Fees

Conveyancing fees vary. However, the charges may be more if the land is registered than if it is unregistered. The average conveyancing fee is about £400. You may have to pay for extra services on top of the fees and VAT will be added. Always agree fees in advance. They tend to rise for homes worth more. The fees should include local authority searches and Land Registry fees.

Survey Costs

These vary from about £250 for a valuation report (a very basic survey) to around £400 for a homebuyer's survey and upwards of £400 for a full structural survey.

Removal Costs

As a first-time buyer you may have little furniture to move so the cheapest way will be to hire a van and do it yourself.

Mortgage Indemnity Guarantee (MIG)

As discussed earlier (pages 47–50), this can often add between £600 and £1000 to the costs of buying a home.

Table 6.1: Typical costs of buying a home

Purchase price	£50,000	£100,000
Solicitor	£333	£416
Land Registry fees	£70	£150
Searches	£79	£79
Stamp duty	Nil	£1000
House purchase report	£265	£340
Total	£747	£1985

Source: Woolwich

Remember that VAT is added to legal/conveyancing fees. Also you may be charged a bank transfer charge when the money is transferred using the CHAPS banking system. These figures exclude the deposit, surveys and removal costs.

Appointing a Solicitor/Conveyancer

Before you start to house hunt, you should also decide on how you will handle your conveyancing and who will handle it for you. This is so that you can inform the estate agent of your solicitor's/conveyancer's details the moment you make an offer and it is accepted. This will speed up the buying process and reduce the risks of being gazumped by another buyer who offers a higher price for the property or who can exchange contracts more quickly.

Conveyancing is the legal act of transferring the right of ownership (the title of the property). It involves checking:

▌ that the vendor really owns the property

▌ that there are no outstanding disputes regarding the property (such as planning disputes)

▌ if there are any covenants attached to the property and that these are not unduly restrictive

■ there are no undisclosed charges or mortgages against the property

■ there is no planning permission in the pipeline that will affect the property

You don't have to employ a solicitor. There are three alternatives:

■ employ a solicitor

■ employ a licensed conveyancer

■ do your own conveyancing

Handling Your Own Conveyancing

Deregulation of the market means that fees have dropped considerably so there is less of a saving if you handle conveyancing yourself.

Fees used to be set at around 1 per cent of the property value, but now can be as low as 0.2 per cent. As such the savings from doing it yourself are often only £300.

If you do handle your own conveyancing your lender is likely to employ its own solicitor to double check your work. You will then have to pay for this. As such the savings are likely to be less than £100 and because of the work/time involved you may find that you lose out on a purchase as a result.

Choosing a Solicitor/Conveyancer

Deregulation of the market means you now have a choice of a solicitor or licensed conveyancer to handle the mechanics of buying your home. A local firm will be better as it will be aware of any local planning applications and even problems with leases or local landlords. As with all aspects of the homebuying process, it pays to shop around.

Often a firm of local estate agents or your lender may be able to recommend a firm of solicitors.

Always agree conveyancing fees in advance. Ask for a written quotation of costs. Remember VAT will be added and there will usually be extras. Ask for a good indication of what these could add up to before employing a solicitor.

Also check that the solicitor can handle the conveyancing quickly and efficiently. You don't want to lose a property because the legal work has delayed the buying process.

7 House Hunting

Location

It may sound like a cliché that estate agents say the three most important factors when choosing a property are 'location, location, location', but it *is* true.

The recent revival in the property market has shown marked differences in price rises, with some areas barely seeing prices rise at all and others seeing increases of 10 or 20 per cent.

At the same time, more popular areas suffer less when prices fall. During the slump from the late 1980s to mid-1990s in parts of London's Docklands, property values slumped by up to 50 per cent. Yet in the more established and desirable areas of the capital, such as Chelsea, prices hardly suffered at all.

Although your main priority may be space or a garden, estate agents generally recommend a 'rabbit hutch' in a good location over a larger property in a less desirable area.

Making money may not be your priority, but remember, as a first-time buyer you are only taking your first step on to the property ladder. You will probably want to move again in the next few years and by buying a property in a more desirable area you will find it easier to get a buyer and should make more of a profit to help you trade up to a bigger home.

Where you buy also has a big impact on the quality of your life and how much it costs to live in the property.

Postcodes not only affect the value of your property but also:

▮ the cost of insurance – not just buildings and contents but also motor insurance

▮ council tax

▌ where your children can go to school (there is always good demand for properties near schools that appear at the top of school league tables). If you have a family or are planning one, check the property falls into the right catchment area

▌ and in London in particular, whether or not you can get a parking permit for a particular borough in central London

Prices on different sides of the same street can differ by as much as 10 or 20 per cent as a result. Remember, subtle boundaries often differentiate what is a desirable area and what is not.

In London you can get 15 to 20 per cent more if you are within 10 minutes' walk of an underground station. In central London houses and flats with garaging or off-street parking also carry a premium of at least 10 per cent.

Houses with gardens, or near gardens, parks and good schools, are always in demand.

Spotting the Right Location

You are probably already aware of the most desirable streets in your area. The ones where the properties look well maintained, that are near to facilities and yet quiet always command higher prices than similar properties in less sought after locations.

These areas are likely to be out of your price bracket as a first-time buyer. However, as an alternative you can buy:

▌ on the fringes of the most desirable areas

▌ in up-and-coming areas (however, this often means that until recently the area was a no-go area for homebuyers and you are taking a chance that it will improve)

How To Spot an Up-and-coming Area

These are the areas that estate agents believe will increase in value and popularity in the years ahead. However, as the name implies, they have not yet increased in value and there is no guarantee that they will. Some cynics say estate agents use the phrase to make an undesirable area seem more attractive.

Up-and-coming areas are those which are going to benefit from better transport links – a new tube line, better railway service or new road links. And those where new employers are moving into the area, creating jobs and prosperity.

In urban areas, those that are near to the centre but have yet to become fashionable are also worth looking at. An up-and-coming area is easy to spot by the number of developments by property companies building new homes or converting offices/wharfs. A large number of skips as homeowners renovate run-down older properties is also a good sign.

Setting Your Priorities

Most homebuyers rely on gut instinct rather than rational reasons when buying a home.

Location remains the most important factor for four out of five homebuyers and nearly 80 per cent decide to buy a home within a matter of seconds after walking through the front door. To stop yourself from making a rash decision based on appearances alone, you should make a list of your priorities.

These will vary from buyer to buyer depending on needs and taste. However, after price the following are likely to be priorities:

- near good quality transport links

- good local amenities such as late-night shops, supermarkets, cinemas, bars and restaurants, and if you have children, good schools

- enough space – many first-time buyers prefer an extra room so they can rent it out if they are strapped for cash

- style of property – either a flat in a Victorian conversion or a modern, hassle-free home

■ car parking – either in a garage or easy street parking

■ similar people to yourself – you may not enjoy living in an area full of retired couples and will probably have more fun in an area favoured by young first- and second-time buyers

■ security – as you will be out at work all day your home is more at risk of being burgled. Don't pick a property next to a crime-ridden council estate and check there is good street lighting and adequate security features on the property

■ garden, patio or balcony

■ near or overlooking a park or other open space or water

■ low running/maintenance costs

Remember, it is unlikely that you will find a property that meets all of these criteria. Six out of ten is normally the compromise you will have to reach.

What Each of Us Looks For in a Property

As with most things in life, there is a difference in the sexes: men tend to look at size and price and women at finish and ambience. Estate agents find that it is easier to sell to men as they tend not to look at the practicalities. So if you are a man bear that in mind. Women, on the other hand, are less likely to take a reduction in the asking price – so bear that in mind if you are buying from a woman.

So, although you have made a list of your priorities, when viewing a property this is what will – according to one recent survey – actually sway your mind.

Men:

Square footage
Address
High ceilings
Room for big sofas

Price
Shower
Unusual properties with
    exposed brick or gadgets

Men:

Large reception room with fireplace

Big hallway (for golf clubs, skis, etc)

Women:

Crisp and clean

A garden

Dressing room

Practical lay-out

Dining area

Ambience and location

Good security

Plenty of good quality cupboards

Sunlight and views

Well-equipped kitchen

Comfort

Different Types of Property

The chances are that you are simply looking for a flat or a starter home you can afford in a suitable area.

But you may also have a set idea of the type of property you want to buy. You may want a light airy flat in a converted period property, or a modern starter home that is fully fitted and easy to maintain.

The property may be leasehold or freehold. It could be old, modern or newly built. It may be fully modernized or need extensive work. The type of property you want to buy will affect the buying process and, once you move in, the running costs.

Leasehold or Freehold

These are the two main types of property ownership: leasehold and freehold.

Leasehold

Generally, if you are buying a flat or, in some cases, a house on an estate you will become a leaseholder. When you buy a leasehold property you purchase a lease for a set number of years – from as little as 10 to as many as 999.

Once the term of the lease has finished, you no longer own the property. As a result, properties with shorter leases are worth less than those with longer ones. Most mortgage lenders will not advance mortgages on properties that have leases with less than 50 years to run as, when the lease starts to run out, these properties can be difficult to resell.

If you buy a leasehold property you will have to pay:

▌ ground rent

▌ service charges

Ground rents are usually low, but you should ask your solicitor to check if they can be increased in future. There have been horror stories of leaseholders threatened with rent rises from £120 to £4160 a year. Hundreds of other leaseholders face similar increases as rents paid under leases granted in the early 1970s come up for their 25-year review. In some cases, leaseholders may be offered the chance to buy the freehold of their property. However, the price of the freehold will take into account the higher ground rent the landlord will be charging and, therefore, will be higher.

Service charges can easily add up to over £100 a month on flats and can rise sharply. The service charge usually includes: buildings insurance, maintenance of the building, cleaning and lighting of communal areas and a 'sinking fund' to pay for major repairs such as a new roof or repainting.

£ CASH TIP £

Check if any major repairs are planned on a leasehold property as you may find that the seller wants to move out before having to chip in several thousand pounds to pay for these. Also, check if service charges are due to rise, how often they rise, if there is a 'sinking fund' to cover major repairs and if other leaseholders are happy with the quality of management.

> **Warning:** If you fail to pay your service charges your property can be repossessed, even if you have managed to keep up-to-date on your mortgage repayments.

> **Warning:** When you move into a leasehold property check that the previous owner is up-to-date on all service charge and ground rent payments.

> **Warning:** There have been horror stories about unscrupulous landlords charging leaseholders exorbitant service charges to cover maintenance and repairs. The freeholder can also make life difficult by deciding to build an extra flat on the roof or extend the property, by failing to maintain the property adequately or by trying to force leaseholders to move out so that the property can be redeveloped. It is advisable to ask other leaseholders (not just the vendor) about the freeholder and management company.

The lease will also have restrictions placed on the use of the property. For instance:

- a requirement that you must redecorate every three or five years

- a restriction on noise after 11pm

- a requirement to dispose of rubbish on a certain date or in a certain way

▌ a ban on pets

▌ a restriction on what you can use the property for

Dealing with problems

If you are in dispute with your landlord over high service charge bills, poor management or shoddy repairs you can take your case to the new network of eight Leasehold Valuation Tribunals which were set up in September 1997.

The new tribunals have the power to settle disputes over service charges and insurance, to look into disagreements over proposed building works and – if the tribunals decide the existing management is unsatisfactory – to appoint new managers to run blocks of flats. The decisions of the tribunals are legally enforceable, although there is an appeals procedure. The tribunals will deal with disputes for a fixed fee. Under the old system only county courts could deal with service charge disputes. However, the drawback of that system was that the courts could award costs. So if the leaseholders lost the case, they could face large bills for their landlord's legal costs.

The Department of the Environment, Transport and the Regions (DETR) has produced a free booklet *Applying to a Leasehold Valuation Tribunal*. It is available from DETR, PO Box no 236, Wetherby L523 7NB, or telephone 0870 1226 236 or fax 0870 1226 237.

Short-lease properties

If you are looking for a central London location the only property you may be able to afford is a short-leasehold property. Provided these are enfranchisable under the 1993 Leasehold Reform Act they can be good value, but you must be prepared for a long battle if you want to buy the freehold.

Mortgage lenders are unlikely to lend on a property with a lease of less than 50 or 60 years. As a result, short leaseholds tend to be far cheaper than freeholds or properties with longer leases. So you will need either a substantial deposit or to be able to afford to buy the property outright as you may not be able to get a mortgage.

Short leaseholds (as with freeholds) are usually fully repairing, which means that if the property is in poor condition you could find yourself with a huge bill for dilapidations. Or else you may face crippling service charges.

Extending the lease/buying the freehold

In many cases leaseholders have a legal right to buy the freehold or extend their lease. The rules are different for houses and flats.

Houses
Under the Leasehold Reform Act 1967 (as amended) most lease-holders have the right to buy the freehold if they have lived in the same house for at least three years. There are other qualifying conditions and some exemptions to this right. The requirement that the ground rent should exceed a certain amount, the so called 'low rent test', now only applies where the original length of the lease is 35 years or less and to certain houses in designated rural areas.

The 1967 Act also gives many leaseholders the right to extend their lease for 50 years without paying a premium. But the ground rent is likely to increase considerably once the extension has started, the right to buy the freehold is lost and there is no right to a further extension.

Flats
Under the Leasehold Reform, Housing and Urban Development Act 1993 (as amended) leaseholders of flats have the right to club together and buy the freehold of their block collectively. Lease-holders generally have to form a company to purchase the free-hold. It can be difficult to get a sufficient number of leaseholders to participate and there are a number of qualifying conditions, including a residence requirement, which can be difficult to meet.

The 1993 Act also gives leaseholders an individual right to renew their lease for a further 90 years once they have lived in their flat for at least three years. A premium is payable but the require-ment to pay ground rent is removed.

In each case, if leaseholders cannot agree a price for buying the freehold or renewing their lease with their landlord, they can apply to a Leasehold Valuation Tribunal which will determine the price. Prices depend on a number of factors but will generally increase as the term of the existing lease gets shorter.

The Department of Environment produces two booklets – *Leasehold Houses* and *Leasehold Flats* – which provide further guidance on the above rights, available from Transport and the Regions.

The government is committed to major reforms of residential leasehold law in England and Wales. In particular it is proposed to simplify the qualifying conditions for the right to buy freeholds. At the time of writing it is not possible to indicate the likely detail of these changes or when they may take effect.

Freehold

If you buy a house this will generally be on a freehold basis. This means that you have bought the absolute ownership of the property and the land on which it stands.

The advantages are that you do not have to pay service charges or ground rent. However, you will have to pay for all repairs and maintenance to the property.

New or Old?

Despite the incentives offered by builders, older homes are increasingly popular with first-time buyers. A recent survey by the Halifax found that only a quarter of first-time buyers prefer a brand new home to a period property (built before 1945). Older homes are preferred because of their character, the fact that they are less uniform and are perceived to be better built. Even though new houses are efficiently heated, insulated, have modern plumbing and are easier to maintain and clean, the average homebuyer prefers to have sash windows (even if they are slighty draughty) and period features (even if that means poor plumbing and extra maintenance).

Part of the attraction is that older homes tend to be cheaper than new homes. The average price of a new built home is £105,711 (at the end of 1998) compared with £81,613 for an older property, according to the Land Registry. And not only are older homes cheaper, but they tend to be more spacious.

New Built

Buying from a builder can have its advantages:

▌ The price often includes extras such as a brand new fitted kitchen, curtains and carpets, and often builders will offer a special deal on a starter pack of furniture. At a time when you are strapped for cash this is a major advantage.

▌ Everything is brand new – you will not have to worry about an ancient boiler breaking down or replacing the kitchen or bathroom in a few years' time.

▌ You will not have to redecorate – and may even have a choice of colours of wallpaper and carpets and the type/colour of fixtures and fittings.

▌ You will not be involved in a chain – the vendor (in this case the builder) does not have to find another property to move into.

▌ There is less chance that you will be gazumped. Once you have seen a property and paid the deposit, you generally know that the property will be yours.

▌ The move will be easier to plan as you usually know exactly when you will be able to move in.

▌ New homes are usually guaranteed by the National House Building Council (NHBC) against structural defects in the first ten years. And for the first two years after the property has been built all defects in building work have to be put right by the builder at no cost to the buyer.

▌ You don't need to pay for the more expensive full structural survey.

▌ Running costs should be lower because newer homes are better insulated and do not need so much maintenance.

▌ You may also be offered a larger mortgage than you would be able to get from a bank or building society as some builders offer 100 per cent home loans. However, watch out for the mortgage rate – it could be higher as a result.

However, there can be drawbacks:

▌ Because new-built homes include extras such as a new kitchen and curtains and carpets, once you move in these then become second hand. As such the property value can fall initially to reflect this. This can be a problem if you want to sell shortly after moving in and new homes are still being built in the area. After all, if you can buy brand new for the same price, there is no point in buying second hand.

▌ Newer homes tend to be built on new estates which often don't have the same facilities – such as a corner shop or local pub – as more established areas.

▌ You may have to sacrifice some of the 'character' – older properties may boast high ceilings, period features and large windows.

▌ Room sizes are often smaller than with older properties.

▌ There may be delays in building schedules so you could find that you have to find temporary accommodation while waiting for building work to be completed.

Warning: If you buy a new home make sure you report any defects in the quality of workmanship to the builders within the first two years, as after this only structural defects are covered by the NHBC warranty. So if doors or windows warp or don't fit properly, put your complaint in writing as soon as possible. Most new homes have minor problems so you must be prepared for these.

Buying Off Plan

The recent strength in the property market means that, increasingly, homebuyers have been purchasing properties before they are even built. Buyers view a show flat which gives an idea of what the property will look like and then pay a deposit on the particular house or flat that they want to buy. Buying usually involves:

▌ viewing a show flat

▌ selecting a flat from a plan which shows its square footage and the size of rooms

The advantages are:

▌ If prices are rising you could make a profit before you even move in because the price you have agreed to pay is less than the market value a few months later when building work is completed.

▌ You have plenty of time in which to plan your move.

▌ You are often given a choice of colour schemes and can even have a say in how the kitchen is designed or where you want light fittings or electrical sockets to be placed.

The disadvantages are:

▌ You will not have a true idea of how the property will look.

▌ If building work is delayed you may have to find temporary accommodation until it is completed.

▌ Show flats are carefully designed to make them appear larger and lighter. Often the beds, sofas and other furnishings are quite small to make rooms seem larger and once you move in your clutter, you may find the flat is much smaller than you first imagined. Some of the bedrooms may not be large enough to accommodate a double wardrobe – or even a double bed.

Warning: Before parting with a deposit read the terms and conditions very carefully. If you have to pull out of the purchase you are unlikely to get your deposit refunded.

£ CASH TIP £

Several buyers have bought off plan and then sold the flat/house without ever moving in. If the property market is rising and prices increase in the time it takes to build the property, this is a way to make a few thousand pounds to finance your next purchase. However, there are pitfalls. You should be prepared to move into the property – once it is built prices could fall or you may not be able to find a buyer. And because most properties are now worth more on completion, some builders are reluctant to sell off plan. The other problem when prices are rising is that developers sometimes realize that they can sell the property for far more than originally agreed and may try to return your deposit so that they can make a bigger profit.

Older Properties

Britain has the oldest stock of homes in Europe, with one in four properties built before the end of the First World War. Many of these have already been renovated, but there is still scope to buy an older home in need of improvement.

The advantages are:

▪ Older properties tend to have higher ceilings, larger room sizes and bigger windows.

▪ The property will be in an established area – so you will know what the area is like and will usually benefit from local shops, restaurants and bars.

▌ The property will usually have more character.

▌ You may be able to improve the property to enhance its value.

The disadvantages are:

▌ The seller may be involved in a chain – trying to find, exchange and complete on another property – and in turn that vendor will have to do the same. This can make moving fraught and as such it may take you several attempts (with all the costs involved) to find a home that you can move into.

▌ The running and maintenance costs are usually higher.

▌ You will have to pay for a full or more detailed survey.

▌ You will have to put up with the taste of the previous owner (even if this is only until you have time to redecorate).

▌ You run the risk of expensive bills in future to replace things like the boiler or fridge or to repair rotten sash windows or a leaking roof.

Conversions

These are often a mixture of the old and the new. Large older homes are often divided into several flats, and during the conversion extensive modernization may mean that the flat appears like new.

The advantages are:

▌ You get the period features of an older property, but with a modern or new bathroom and kitchen.

▌ In more established areas where prices are high, you will probably not be able to stretch to buying a whole house. A conversion may enable you to afford the area of your choice.

The disadvantage is:

▌ Much depends on the quality of the conversion. These large homes were not designed for multiple occupancy. As such you may be able to hear your neighbours walking around upstairs or you may find that your plasterboard walls offer little privacy.

Former Offices/Industrial Buildings

Converting office blocks that are no longer needed for commercial purposes into residential apartments is increasingly popular in and around inner cities. Already, many wharf and water-side buildings have been converted into flats in London, Manchester and Liverpool.

The advantages of these are that:

▌ they are usually centrally located, cutting down on commuting time

▌ they often offer more space than comparable flats

▌ concrete floors and solid walls usually mean they are quieter than conversions of residential properties

▌ these homes are usually highly desirable so you should find them easy to resell

▌ you can often buy properties in 'shell' form – you can then design the interior to suit your tastes and needs.

The disadvantages are:

▌ because these properties are desirable they are often very expensive

▌ you often have to pay out substantial sums after moving in to pay for curtains, carpets and decoration; with 'shell' properties you will also have to pay for plumbing, wiring, kitchens and bathrooms and the building of internal walls.

Lofts

These New York style open plan industrial flats started to become fashionable in London at the end of the 1980s and are now popular in most urban areas.

True lofts are converted old industrial buildings. However, loft-style apartments are now being built from scratch and offices, schools and even churches are being converted.

Generally, it is the quality of the building conversion – rather than the individual lofts – that affects the price. The exterior, windows, security and maintenance of the building will affect its long-term value more than decoration.

If you are buying a 'shell' apartment – which means you must build the interior including walls, and install plumbing, kitchens, wiring and bathrooms from scratch – you will need to ensure you have enough finance to cover these costs. A lender is only likely to lend on the basis that you can afford to turn the shell into a home. Basic fitting costs around £40 to £50 a square foot, although the sky is the limit. Building something unusual can either attract buyers or put them off and there is less of a chance that you will appeal to the maximum number of buyers.

Former Council Flats/Houses

Tenants who bought through the Right to Buy scheme introduced by the Conservative Government in 1979 are now beginning to sell these council homes.

Although these tend to be far cheaper than other similar properties in an area, which may make them attractive for those who cannot afford anything else, there are some drawbacks.

The main problem is finance as many lenders are reluctant to advance mortgages on former council flats, because they can be hard to sell.

Another drawback can be the fact that the local council is the freeholder and therefore is responsible for repairs, service charges and maintenance of the estate/block. As such, the council is unlikely to pay for anything other than essential repairs – 24-hour porterage, a well stocked private garden and interior designed communal areas are something you are going to have to live without.

Before buying check:

▊ How many flats/houses are already privately owned. Buying in a block or on an estate where there are a high number of owner occupiers will help when it comes to selling the property.

▊ What plans the council has for the building. Remember, as with other leasehold properties you will have to pay service charges. So if extensive work is planned, you could face a huge increase in service charges. If there are only a few owner occupiers the service charges can be very high.

▊ If the block/house is in a good area or surrounded by run-down, high-rise, poor quality housing. Pick the block and area carefully. As with all property purchases, location is the key.

Remember:

▊ Low-rise flats are easier to sell than high-rise.

▊ Ex-council homes can be difficult to resell.

▊ Security is important. A flat in a block that has a bad reputation for crime and vandalism will be very difficult to resell.

▊ Maintenance is another key factor. If you buy in a block where the lift is constantly breaking down or the grounds are strewn with rubbish and old furniture you will find it very difficult to sell your property.

Buying a Run-down Property

With a large number of homes in the UK falling below the government's tolerable standards, there is still plenty of scope to make money out of renovating an older property.

Remember, the costs of renovating a property quickly mount up to more than you budgeted for, take longer and are far more stressful. Often you will be better off paying more and having to do less work. What may be a profitable conversion for a builder could turn out to be unprofitable for the ordinary homebuyer.

There is often a very good reason why properties are cheap. Many run-down properties have been repossessed by mortgage lenders and may have either been left empty for several months or not benefited from maintenance and repairs because the cash-strapped homeowner could not afford these. In other cases, those faced with repossession strip their homes of everything from the bath to the kitchen to sell and raise much needed cash.

Repossessions have been plentiful in the past few years, but the number is drying up and has now dropped to the lowest level since the first half of 1990. Even so there were some 32,000 repossessions in 1998.

They are sold either through estate agents, if they are in reasonable condition, or through residential property auctioneers.

If you are buying a property 'in need of modernization' or 'with room for improvement' always pay for a full structural survey and ask the surveyor to investigate specific areas of concern such as the roof or foundations.

Investigate how easy it will be to get planning consent. Then get accurate estimates for how much work will cost (and add another 10 per cent for contingencies). If the costs outweigh the additional value that will be added to the property, think again.

Warning: If a property is in need of even minor works – such as new guttering – the mortgage lender may withhold part of the mortgage advance until this work is completed, and give you either three or six months in which to prove that the work has been done to a satisfactory standard. If money is retained in this way you will not only have to find extra cash to meet the mortgage shortfall but will also have to pay for the repairs.

Finding a Property

The term 'house hunting' has never been more apt than in today's market. With as many as a dozen buyers after each property for sale, you will have to learn to hunt for a suitable property. And with gazumping (where another buyer snatches a property from you at the last minute by offering a higher price) you will also have to learn the hunter's instincts – be cunning, outwit your prey and be patient.

Approaching Estate Agents

Once you have decided what type of property you want, what you can afford and where you want to buy, approach as many estate agents as you can in the areas concerned. You may find that only a few specialize in the type or price of property that you are interested in.

With more potential buyers than there are sellers in most parts of the country, agents are reluctant to waste time on those who are 'just looking' and will favour those who are genuine buyers, so stress the following:

▪ you are serious about buying

▪ you are a first-time buyer and as such are not in a chain (you will not have to find a buyer for your existing home)

- you have mortgage finance in place so can move quickly (ask your lender to agree a mortgage for a certain amount 'in principle')

- you are keen to move quickly and can view properties at short notice

Try and establish a good rapport with the estate agent – that way he or she will think of you first when a property comes on to the market. Then tell the estate agent:

- How much you can afford, and don't say you can offer more if you can't.

- What you are looking for – you don't want to waste your own or the estate agent's time by viewing unsuitable properties. But don't be too specific. Remember you are unlikely to find a property that meets all your criteria within your price bracket.

- How to get in touch with you at short notice (your work/home and mobile phone numbers). If you have access to a fax, ask if property details can be faxed to you rather than posted, to ensure you are one of the first to see a property.

Then keep in contact with the estate agent on a regular basis:

- Ask the estate agent to inform you of any sales that have fallen through. The seller may be fed up and, if you are prepared to act quickly, you could find that you can move in a couple of weeks.

- Keep pestering the estate agent to find out if there are any new properties coming on to his or her books. In areas where the number of buyers far outstrips the number of sellers, there is no point in asking the estate agent to ring you back. They are far too busy. It is up to you to ring them.

- Don't waste the estate agent's time by asking to see properties you are not interested in. The agent may think you are not serious about buying and may be reluctant to show you properties in future, particularly if there is a queue of serious buyers prepared to put in sensible offers.

▌ If a property comes on to the market, push to see the property that day – otherwise you may find that it is 'under offer' before you find time to view it.

Property particulars

Once you have registered on their books, estate agents will then send you property details. It is essential that you respond to these as soon as possible. In the current market you may find that the property is already under offer (a price has been agreed) before you receive the particulars. That is why it is essential to telephone estate agents on a regular basis.

Under the Property Misdescriptions Act, what estate agents can say on property particulars is strictly regulated. The Act prevents estate agents from lying or giving false information about a property.

There will usually be a brief *description* of the type of property (flat or house), its age and location as well as whether it is leasehold or freehold. Other information that may be included is: council tax, length of lease, service charges/ground rent and whether it is in good repair or in need of renovation.

Measurements should be accurate (they cannot add a couple of feet on to the size of a room) and are usually expressed as follows: 'living room 20ft × 16ft'. If the measurement says 'maximum' this means that the room is that large at its widest or longest point. So if it is L-shaped or has an alcove or bay window the room may be much smaller than the maximum measurements indicate.

The details will also include the *price*. If it is listed as 'ono' – this means 'or near offer' – you may have scope to offer less than the asking price.

The Act also requires estate agents to inform you if they have a personal interest in a property.

But while the Act requires estate agents to be honest, it does not require them to inform you of every defect with the property. You won't see property details saying 'desirable two bedroom flat, slight damp problem, roof leaks when it rains and the boiler is on its last legs'. Remember the estate agent is employed to present the property in the best light. And while agents must be truthful about things like distances and journey times, they are likely to verge on the side of optimism. So if a property is 10 minutes walk from the station, you may find it takes you 15 or 20 minutes. And a 30-minute train journey from the nearest town or city may be 30 minutes only on a fast train.

However, if you ask (preferably in writing) a specific question about a property, the estate agent must give you an honest answer. Vendors, on the other hand, can lie – so don't take their word for anything. Remember the golden rule is *caveat emptor*, or buyer beware.

The Act does not prevent estate agents from using their own terminology to describe a home. Property particulars nearly always begin with 'spectacular', 'spacious', 'charming', 'stunning' or another flattering phrase.

Although estate agents have toned down the more misleading euphemisms, they still use terms like:

'Scope for improvement' – a lot of work will be needed so you will either need a lot of money or be a DIY enthusiast
'Much sought after' – either it will probably be sold before you get to view it or the estate agent wants you to think that it will
'Requires modernization' – does not have central heating and maybe even still has an outside loo
'Cottage' – small
'Bijou' – even smaller
'Near station' – trains run at the back of your garden
'Convenient for local bars and restaurants' – it's next door to a noisy pub
'Light and airy' – lots of large draughty windows

The key to reading property particulars is to look at what they don't say. If service charges are not mentioned, does that mean they are so high they may be offputting? And read between the lines. If you are sent details about a fifth floor flat, why isn't the lift mentioned? Perhaps there isn't one. Remember that while a photograph may be enclosed, it may be taken from a very flattering angle or cropped (the tower block on the left may no longer be visible).

Problems with estate agents

A few estate agents have been accused of accepting payments from buyers desperate to secure a deal on a property and avoid being gazumped. Under the National Association of Estate Agents' code, estate agents are not allowed to accept payments from buyers as well as sellers. However, if the agent is acting only for a buyer a homefinder's fee can be paid.

The other reported scam is for agents to inform buyers that there have been higher offers made on the property. These turn out to be fictitious, but as agents work on a commission basis they have every incentive to push the price higher.

If you have exhausted your estate agent's complaints procedure and are still not happy, contact the Ombudsman for Estate Agents on 01722 333306. They can award compensation of up to £50,000 if they rule in favour of the complainant. The most paid out to date is £13,000. But note: not every estate agent is a member of the Ombudsman Scheme, so check first.

Other Ways To Find a Property

Although using an estate agent is likely to be the best option – after all you don't have to pay the commission and as such the service costs you nothing – there are other ways to find a property.

Advertisements in papers

Your local paper will be the ideal place to find out about new property developments. Most papers run a weekly property section or page with a mixture of editorial and advertisements.

Builders often advertise their new developments in papers rather than selling through estate agents. The adverts will tell you about open days (days when you can view the properties) and any special incentives offered (such as 100 per cent home loans or free kitchen appliances).

Private sales – where the vendor does not want the expense of employing an estate agent – are also usually advertised in newspapers.

Using an agent

If you are finding it hard to buy a property you can employ an agent to act on your behalf, paying a fee of between 1.5 and 2 per cent of the purchase price. Although this adds to the cost of buying, agents can often find properties that are not on the open market and the attraction of this arrangement is that the vendor does not have to pay estate agency fees (unless they have already signed up with an estate agent, in which case the agent may insist on still charging the fee).

Buying at auction

As a first-time buyer you may not want to take the risk of buying at auction. Inexperienced househunters usually lose out to the professional property developers who know how to get the best deal. If you do succeed in buying a property it may be because those in the know wouldn't touch such a bad investment.

Pros:
▌ If you are successful you could buy a property for far less than through an estate agent.

▌ You can often buy a more unusual property – such as a former railway station or an old police house.

Cons:
▌ There is often a reason why properties are sold at auction rather than through an estate agent – properties tend to be in much poorer repair, in less desirable areas, may have subsidence or are uninsurable, may be in a noisy area or have a restrictive lease. Squatters may have left the property in a poor state or it may be a repossession that has been left empty for several months. If this is the case then you may find it hard to get a mortgage.

▌ You should pay for a survey, legal searches and a valuation before making your bid, but could find this money is wasted because you have been outbid.

▌ If the property needs extensive work you should also find out about any planning requirements you will need to meet.

How to buy at auction: The first rule is don't. If you have found a property you want to buy, ask the vendors if they are willing to sell prior to the auction. If this isn't an option, apply the following rules:

▌ Sign up with as many auctioneers as possible.

▌ If you see a property that appeals in a catalogue, ask the auctioneer for all the information about that property.

▌ Find out the guide price from the auctioneer – this will be close to the reserve price and will give you an indication of how much you are likely to have to pay.

▌ Look over the property yourself.

▌ Keep in touch with the auctioneer to check that the property is still for sale. You don't want to pay out for survey and legal fees, only to find that the property has been withdrawn from the auction.

▌ Arrange your finance. You can usually apply for a mortgage and receive an agreement in principle. The lender will require a valuation by an approved valuer, a survey (a full survey in most cases) and legal and planning searches in advance. Remember, you will have to pay these fees even if the sale falls through. You may find that the property is in such poor repair that it is unmortgageable. Also, remember to budget for the 10 per cent deposit, legal and professional fees, stamp duty and the cost of repairs.

▌ You should instruct a solicitor to handle the conveyancing and searches as you will have to give the solicitor's name and address to the auctioneer if your bid is accepted.

▌ Contact an insurer to find out if there will be any problems insuring the property.

At the auction:

▌ Get there early to find out if there are any last minute changes.

▌ Set yourself a maximum bidding limit – so you don't get carried away and bid more than you can afford.

▌ If your bid is accepted, you will usually be required to pay a 10 per cent deposit immediately the bid is accepted. You will then have 28 days to pay the final balance. Find out what form of payment the auctioneer accepts.

▌ Remember, if your bid is accepted you have entered into a binding contract.

▌ Leasehold properties require a detailed study of the lease with solicitors' advice.

▌ If the property is a repossession you must also check that you are not liable for any unpaid ground rents or service charges.

For further information: The Incorporated Society of Valuers and Auctioneers, 3 Cadogan Gate, London, SW1X 0AS (telephone 020 7235 2282) produces a leaflet giving guidelines for anyone buying or selling their home at auction.

Viewing a Property

Once you have been sent property particulars by estate agents (or seen a property advertised in a newspaper), you then move on to the next stage in the house hunting process.

As a first-time buyer it is essential that you don't buy the first property you see unless it really is your ideal home. You should view a few properties just so that you get to know what is on offer.

You must make an appointment to view with the estate agent. If you are one of the first to view you will have a better chance of making the first offer that is accepted.

The estate agent will often come with you to view the property (particularly on the first viewing) or may arrange for you to view when the vendors are at home.

Remember, you can view a property more than once. If you are interested in the property – or have already made an offer – you can view again to check that your first impressions were right or to measure up to see if your furniture will fit.

If you cannot make an appointment make sure you cancel in plenty of time. If you don't, you will annoy the estate agent and the vendor.

When To View

If you can, drive past the property and view it from the outside on different days of the week and at different times. That way you can find out what the early morning or late evening traffic is like and if it is a 'rat run', how easy it is to park the car at night, if there are any noisy neighbours and if the trains/buses/tubes that run nearby make so much noise you cannot sleep at night.

Viewing at different times will also let you see how light affects the property. You may find that even on a sunny morning the property looks dark and dingy or that the garden never gets any sun because of overlooking properties. Things to look out for include:

▌ Nearby pubs, cinemas, sports grounds, restaurants or other entertainment facilities that could cause problems with noise, rubbish, congestion and parking.

▌ Nearby houses that are unkempt or derelict – they could affect local property values or, worse, become squats.

▌ Nearby properties with cracks in the brickwork – this could be an indication that the area suffers from subsidence.

▌ Street lighting – is the area well lit and safe to walk around at night?

▌ Are there any large trees near the property? These could cause subsidence.

▌ Is the property exposed or secluded?

▌ Are there any geographical features that could affect the property – if it is on a steep hill will you want to walk up it every night after a hard day's work; are there any streams or rivers that could cause flooding?

What to Take

When viewing a property, take with you the estate agent's particulars, a notepad and pen and a tape measure. The tape measure is so you can check your sofa/bed/wardrobe/bookshelves will fit into a particular space. It will also be useful to check the estate agent's details – these are often given as maximum dimensions or as an overall square footage.

Also make up a list of questions you want to ask or points you want to check. For instance:

▌ Will the carpets and curtains be included in the sale?

▌ What type of central heating system is installed and how old is it?

▌ What items of kitchen equipment will be sold with the property – it is usual for fitted cookers to be included, but not always fridges, dishwashers or washing machines.

A more detailed list is included in the section on 'Conveyancing – what questions to ask'.

Viewing from Outside

Most people make up their mind whether or not they will buy a property in a matter of minutes. Viewing the property from outside will give you a good indication of whether or not this is the type of property you will be interested in buying.

You should also take a few minutes to look at the following:

▌ the state of the roof

▌ whether or not there are any obvious cracks in the walls (indications of subsidence)

▌ the state of repair of the windows

▌ the quality of security (if it is a block of flats, is the communal front door kept locked?)

▌ parking facilities or availability of street parking

▌ state of repair of party walls/fences or communal gardens/walkways

Viewing Inside the Property

First impressions can often be misleading. Don't be put off by the existing owner's decor – you can always change that. Or you may feel that this is the perfect property only to find that when you move in there is not enough storage space.

If you are looking inside a new home or show flat, the furniture may be arranged to give the illusion that the property is larger than it is. When you move in a king-size bed you may find there is no room in the bedroom for anything else.

The following are often overlooked:

▌ Light – is there enough natural light and where does the sun shine into the flat/house and at what time of day?

▌ Storage – is there somewhere to store your suitcases/bicycle/filing cabinet?

▌ Wardrobes – are these fitted or will you have to buy your own and, if so, is there enough room?

▌ Noise – can you hear the neighbours/cars driving past the property? If the walls are made of plasterboard you may find that you have little privacy within the property.

▌ Central heating – what type is it, how long has it been installed and are there sufficient radiators? Remember that what seems a light and airy home in summer can be a dark and cold place in the winter.

▌ Electrical fittings – are there enough electrical sockets and are they conveniently placed?

▌ Kitchen – is it practical? Could you actually cook a meal in it, is there adequate ventilation, is there enough space to fit a washing machine and a tumble dryer and if you are planning to live with someone else can you both fit in the kitchen at the same time?

▌ Dining – is there somewhere to eat? Is there enough room to entertain?

▌ Plumbing – turn on a couple of taps (or ask to use the bathroom) to find out if the plumbing is noisy and if the hot water works.

▌ Laundry – is there a washing machine, will it be left by the present owners, is there somewhere to dry/air clothes?

▌ Bathroom – is there a shower or room to fit a power shower? Is there enough room to store towels and toiletries?

▌ Neighbours – it is very difficult to find out if there are problem neighbours before buying a property. But it is worth doing a bit of detective work as you could end up living in misery because of loud music, a noisy dog or damp because your neighbour has failed to maintain his or her property. Yet only 16 per cent of buyers are worried about their future neighbours, even though they can make life hell and affect the future saleability of the property.

Other Things to Consider

Repair costs: Look for items that might be expensive to repair: windows, floors, roof, electrics, damp, central heating and cracks in the walls.

Running costs: Few homebuyers check the running costs of the property, but these can often mean the difference between easily affording to buy and struggling. Costs to consider include:

- heating – large draughty rooms and rotting or ill-fitting windows can make heating bills soar and leave you in a cold unwelcoming home in winter

- council tax

- insurance – some postcode areas are very expensive because of high crime rates or increased risks of subsidence

- service charges and ground rent if you are buying a leasehold property

Living costs: If you move far away from work your travelling costs can easily mount up and if there are no local supermarkets you may find that buying your food at the local corner shop works out to be very expensive.

8 Once You Have Found a Property: Offers, Searches, Valuations and Surveys

Making an Offer

If, after viewing a property, you decide you want to buy it, make your decision quickly. If you dither you may find that someone else has already made an offer that has been accepted or you could be gazumped.

Before making an offer remember this: *Buy with your brain not your heart.* Ask yourself:

▌ Do I really want to live there?

▌ Could I cope with commuting from that distance?

▌ Can I really afford to live there? Remember running costs as well as purchase costs.

▌ Does the property meet most of my requirements?

If you want to make an offer tell the estate agent and ask to be informed as soon as possible if your offer has been accepted. You must inform the estate agent, not the vendor, so that the agent can tell other potential buyers that the property is under offer and stop showing other potential buyers round the property.

In the current property market you may not be able to offer much less than the asking price – but you can try. Be prepared for the vendor to refuse the offer, so that you may have to come back with a higher offer.

When you make an offer and it is accepted, this is not a binding contract (other than in Scotland). Either you – or the vendor – can pull out of the agreement at any time until exchange of contracts. This is when you pay a deposit on the property and the sale is confirmed.

So when you make an offer make sure it is 'subject to contract'. This means you can pull out if:

▌ the survey shows that the property is in a poor condition (for instance it is suffering from damp or subsidence) or needs extensive work. In this case you can either withdraw your offer or make a lower offer.

▌ you are unable to raise the required mortgage.

▌ the local authority searches show that the property value and your enjoyment of the property may be affected in some way – for instance a major road will be built through your back garden.

▌ you simply change your mind.

Making an offer 'subject to contract' gives you no protection against being gazumped or the vendor pulling out of the sale – which could cost you up to £1000 in wasted legal and surveying fees. But it does have its compensations. This system protects you from being committed to buying a property that later turns out to be suffering from major problems. So if the vendor objects to agreeing to a purchase on a 'subject to contract' basis be wary. Do not sign any contract at this stage of the buying process without taking legal advice.

If your offer is accepted set an early date for exchange of contracts, to avoid the risk of being gazumped.

To protect yourself against the financial loss of being gazumped, you can take out insurance. Legal and General and the Lambeth Building Society both have policies costing from £15 to £30. (See the section on Gazumping, p.127, for more details on how to protect yourself against gazumping.)

Warning: In the current property market it is easy to be pushed into a panic purchase. One month a property can be on the market for £80,000 and a few months later for £90,000. A lot of these price rises are fuelled by a shortage of properties for sale, not by genuine increases in prices. The shortage means that buyers are forced into offering higher and higher prices to get the property they want. If demand drops as a result of higher mortgage rates or a downturn in the economy, so might the value of the property, so there is a slight risk that you could find yourself with 'negative equity' – where the amount of mortgage debt exceeds the value of the property.

Once Your Offer Has Been Accepted

If your offer is accepted it is important to put pressure on your solicitor, surveyor and estate agent to push the sale through as quickly as possible to avoid the risk of gazumping. Then:

1 Inform your mortgage lender so that:
   - the final amount of loan can be agreed
   - the lender can tell you how to arrange a valuation of the property (this can often be combined with a survey); you may have to use a valuer from a panel approved by the lender
   - a provisional date for the mortgage to be advanced can be agreed
2 Instruct your solicitor to proceed with conveyancing to exchange of contracts:
   - give details of the property address
   - give the name of the vendor's solicitor (ask the estate agent)
   - give details of your mortgage lender
   - tell the solicitor roughly how quickly you wish to proceed and when you expect to move into the property

3 Arrange for a surveyor/valuer to inspect the property.
4 Give notice (if you have not done so already) that you will be moving out of your current accommodation.
5 In some cases you may be required to pay a preliminary deposit (particularly if you are buying from a builder). If the estate agent asks for a deposit (say £250 as a token of your intent) remember that this deposit has no legal standing and does not bind you to the transaction. Make sure you get a receipt and if you sign anything make sure it says the deposit is paid 'subject to contract and to survey'.

£ CASH TIP £

Take out homebuyer legal protection insurance to cover you in case you need to take legal action against the builder of your property, the conveyancers/solicitors, surveyors or the removal firm. The Home Buyer Legal Protection policy (01968 678 989) provides up to £25,000 towards the cost of legal action provided action is started within three years of moving and costs under £40. Alternatively make sure you have legal expenses insurance included in your household insurance policy (see the section on insuring your home in chapter 11). However, this will not cover disputes that started before the policy was taken out (such as problems with your survey).

How Long Will it Take from Making an Offer to Moving In?

With an average 11 buyers viewing each available property in the capital there is intense competition among homebuyers. This puts immense pressure on them to complete the homebuying process as quickly as possible to reduce the risks of gazumping.

The average time between a property being on the market and the final offer is now only one week in some areas of the South East, rising to three weeks in Glasgow and four weeks in some areas of the North East.

The time between the offer being accepted and the exchange of contracts averages 10 to 12 weeks. Once contracts have been exchanged you will then have an average of just three weeks to arrange the move before completion.

Conveyancing: Legal Searches and Checks

What is Conveyancing?

Conveyancing is the legal process by which the right of ownership of the property (the title of the property) is transferred. There are two stages:

- from acceptance of your offer up to exchange of contracts

- from exchange of contracts to completion

Once contracts have been exchanged neither the buyer or seller can pull out. The process can take anything from 48 hours to two months or more.

The first stage involves vital checks, including what is included in the purchase price, whether any planning applications will affect the property and if there are any restrictions on the use of the property. Your solicitor/conveyancer should check the following.

- *The vendor has the right to sell the property* – this will usually be done by checking the Land Registry.

- *The property is not subject to any outstanding undisclosed 'charges'* – this means that no other person or institution has a right to the proceeds of the sale of the property and no loans (other than any mortgage that will be repaid with the proceeds of the sale) are charged against the property.

- *The property is sold with vacant possession* – when the seller leaves it will be empty and ready for you to occupy and there are no 'sitting' tenants.

Your solicitor will also ask the vendor's solicitor to complete a questionnaire which will include the following points:

What is included in the sale: Generally, anything that is part of the fabric of the property is included in the sale, but there can be disputes. It is not unknown for some vendors to remove inbuilt dishwashers, curtain rails, light fittings, fitted cupboards and even fireplaces. The usual rule is that if it is not removable without causing damage it is part of the structure of the property and it is included in the sale. But it is safer to check.

Your solicitor will ask specific questions about many items – these are listed on a standard form which the vendor must complete. However, it may still be advisable to go through the property with the vendor agreeing what is included in the sale shortly after you have made your offer. Put the list in writing and give a copy to your solicitor. If not, make sure that the list of items included and excluded in the sale sent out by your solicitor includes any items that you are specifically interested in ensuring are part of the sale. And don't be fobbed off by replies which say 'see estate agent's particulars' or are vague.

There can be areas of dispute. Check the following:

▌ Kitchen – if there are any free-standing items such as a slot-in cooker, fridge, dishwasher or washing machine, remember these are not always included in the sale.

▌ Wardrobes – usually if they are fitted, they are included in the sale – but not always. If they are part of a matching set of furniture the vendor may want to take them.

▌ Garden – some sellers even go as far as digging up plants. If the greenhouse or garden shed is built on foundations it should be included in the sale.

▌ Carpets – these are usually included in the sale (occasionally vendors ask for an extra amount to pay for these) but rugs are not.

▌ Light fittings – check whether the vendor plans to remove lamp shades (most do) and any light fittings including wall lamps (most don't). Be prepared for some vendors to go as far as removing all the light bulbs.

▌ Curtains – these are often negotiated as a separate sale.

▌ Shelves – if these are to be removed make sure that the vendor 'makes good' any damage to the walls or plaster.

▌ Bathroom fittings – if the bathroom cabinets, towel rails and toilet roll holders are fitted they should generally be included in the sale. However, some vendors do take them with them.

▌ TV aerial – satellite dishes are often removed and occasionally even the TV aerial.

Don't forget to check that the agreed items have been left by the vendor and that the items are still the same and have not been exchanged for cheap, second-hand goods.

Make sure the list of what is included in the sale is agreed early on in the conveyancing procedure as it may affect the price you are prepared to pay for the property or you may have to raise extra cash to pay for curtains and carpets.

Your solicitor or conveyancer will need to know the details of any items in the house which you have agreed to buy as an extra.

It is also not uncommon for buyers to find that they have inherited certain items they do not want. The vendor may leave behind an old wardrobe, shelving units or a dirty old carpet. Make sure you agree that all items of furniture are removed, just in case the vendor has other ideas.

Whether there are any guarantees: Your solicitor or conveyancer should ask if there are any guarantees covering:

▌ the damp course

▌ any treatment for woodrot/woodworm

▌ any items of major work – such as a new roof

▌ the boiler/central heating system

▌ any wiring/plumbing/electrical items, etc

Where the boundaries of the property lie: Boundary disputes can cause major problems and even lead to court cases between neighbours. Don't assume that fences, hedges and walls give a true indication of the boundary of the property.

Your solicitor should give you a plan showing exactly where the boundaries lie and who is responsible for maintaining any boundary walls or fences. Some property deeds can be vague, so make sure you measure carefully to check boundaries are in the correct place.

There may be obligations or conditions specified in the deeds, for instance a minimum or maximum height of any fence, whose responsibility it is to repair any fence or wall or whether or not boundary fences or hedges are allowed.

If there are any restrictive covenants: There may be a restriction on what the property can be used for, that it cannot be let, that no pets may be kept or that you are required to paint the property in a particular colour. Your solicitor/conveyancer should check that these are not unduly restrictive.

That there are no outstanding disputes regarding the property: There could be disputes regarding boundaries or planning applications. The solicitor should also check that any additions to the property – such as an extension – have met local planning requirements and that building regulation consent was obtained.

If there are any rights of way or rights of access: This involves checking that you don't have a public right of way or footpath through the grounds of the property and if you have shared rights of access with a neighbour – for instance to a driveway or garden.

Local Authority Searches

One of the solicitor's or conveyancer's jobs is to request local searches to check that there are no plans in the pipeline that may affect the value or future enjoyment of the home you are buying. If a major road is about to be built near your new home or a large superstore is being built on land nearby you will want to know about it so you can either pull out of the purchase or negotiate a lower price.

Local searches are charged on a flat fee basis and usually cost around £50. However, if you live in an area that may need an extra geological search – for instance if there has been extensive mining in the past – this will cost extra.

There used to be long delays in waiting for local searches to be completed by local authorities, with some taking weeks or even months. The average time today is only a few weeks. If you need to exchange contracts before the search has been completed it is possible to take out an insurance policy to cover you against any negative information the search may have uncovered. Your solicitor/conveyancer should be able to give you details.

In some cases the vendor may request a local authority search at the time of putting the property on the market. This speeds up the process and the costs are eventually borne by the buyer.

Warning: There can be flaws in this process. Local authority searches only cover the property itself and will not show up information about nearby property that may be demolished to make way for a tower block. You may fall in love with a home because of its view but the search may not uncover that this may soon be spoilt by a new development because the land is not near enough to show up on the search.

Remember, when the Channel Tunnel rail link was proposed thousands of homes in London and the South East were blighted, but the proposals did not appear on local authority searches.

Tip: If there is any unused land or there are any derelict properties nearby, you can ask the owners and local residents if they know of any plans for development.

Land Registry Searches

The title of the property is usually checked through the Land Registry, the official register of land ownership. Nine in ten properties are listed on its database. If it is registered the owner will have a Land Certificate (or Charge Certificate if the property is mortgaged). This certificate gives all the information held at the Land Registry including:

▌ a site plan (showing the size and location of the property)

▌ the ownership or proprietorship register

▌ a charges register showing if there are any outstanding rights over the property (for instance a mortgage or loan secured against it)

If the property is not registered, ownership is proved by the production of the title deeds.

The solicitor or conveyancer will also register the transfer of ownership of the property into your name with the Land Registry. The fees for this are paid by the buyer and range from £40 to £500, depending on the value of the property.

Buying a New Property

If you are buying a newly-built home your solicitor/conveyancer should also check:

▌ that the boundaries of the property are as shown on the plan

▌ that the size of the property is as shown

▌ that services are provided/connected

▌ that the contract provides for the house to be properly built to the specification

▌ whether there are any rights of way over the property

- that the local authority has agreed to the construction of roads and, once they are built, will take them over (if the road is not maintained by the council, residents will have to foot the bill)

- whether there are any restrictions – such as the fact that no fences or garden boundaries can be built

- that planning permission was obtained, complied with and did not contain any restrictive conditions

- that drainage and sewerage will be taken over and maintained by the relevant utility.

Leasehold Properties

If you are buying a leasehold property the conveyancing will also involve the transfer of the lease from the vendor to the purchaser. As such your solicitor should check:

- that the lease does not have any restrictions that may affect the value or your future enjoyment of the property

- that the current leaseholder is up-to-date on service charge and ground rent payments

- that there are no problems with the lease that could affect the future saleability of the property

Valuations

Your lender will require a valuation of the property usually by a firm on its approved panel of surveyors. This is to ensure that the property is adequate security for the loan and that the mortgage advance is not greater than the value of the property or greater than a certain percentage of its value (for instance if you are taking out a 95 per cent mortgage).

Warning: The overheating of the property market in some areas means that even if you think the property you are buying is 'worth' the amount you are paying, your lender may not. Valuers were caught out in the 1988 house price boom when they overvalued some properties and, as a result, they are now more conservative. However, it is still unlikely that the lender's valuation will be lower than the price you have offered. If it is you will either have to find the extra cash to meet the shortfall (lenders will only advance mortgages on the amount set by the valuer) or worse, you may have to pull out of the purchase.

Surveys

In more than 80 per cent of purchases, homebuyers rely on the valuation and buy without a thorough survey. They may pay tens or even hundreds of thousands of pounds for a home, but are not prepared to ensure that this investment is sound by spending a few hundred pounds on a full survey.

Unless you are buying a newly-built or recently-built house, or a flat in a modern block, you should consider paying for a survey. If there is a major fault with the building this survey can save you thousands of pounds in the long run. Even if there are only minor faults, a survey can still pay as you may be able to negotiate a reduction in the asking price.

If you fail to have a survey not only will you have little idea of the amount of work that may be required, but may have no means of redress should you find that there are major problems.

'Caveat Emptor' – or Buyer Beware

Agents – but not individuals – are obliged to be truthful when advertising and marketing properties under the Properties Misdescription Act 1991. This may give you some comfort, but if you are not relying on a survey but what the vendor tells you, you could be left seriously out of pocket. Even estate agents are not obliged to disclose more than they feel like disclosing.

So if the estate agent knows there has been a negative survey which led to a potential buyer pulling out, that agent does not have to tell you. However, if you ask you must be told the truth. If the estate agent lies, he or she is breaking the law. However, if you ask the vendors and they lie, you generally have no case.

Different Types of Survey

The valuation report

Sometimes paid for by the lender, it usually costs between £150 and £200. This is a valuation. Although you, as the buyer, must usually pay for it, it is designed to reassure the lender that the property is worth enough to cover the amount of the loan should you default on the mortgage payments.

The valuation report will only outline any serious problems that affect the value of the property. So if the home is suffering from subsidence or damp this should be pointed out.

In a few cases the valuer may value the property at less than the asking or agreed purchase price. As a result, the amount the lender is prepared to lend may be reduced.

If major or substantial repairs are required on the property, the lender will probably withhold a proportion of the mortgage until these works have been completed. Often a time limit – say three or six months – is given in which these repairs or renovations must be carried out.

The homebuyers' survey and valuation

As a rough guide, this costs between £300 and £400. It is more detailed than the valuation report and is often completed at the same time as the valuation and by the same surveyor. However, it is not what is commonly referred to as a 'full survey'. It is also known as the House Purchase and Valuation report, the Home Buyers' Survey and Valuation (HBSV) and a Scheme Two Survey.

The survey is completed on a standard form and is designed to pick up major faults. The survey will also tell you if there are any items of work that you will need to undertake shortly after moving in. Although the report should point out any damp, woodrot or woodworm, the surveyor will probably not inspect under floor-boards or in the roof.

Building or full structural survey

This costs upwards of £400. It is recommended for those buying older properties, conversions of older properties and unusual homes. It can be combined with the valuation, although it is often done separately. You can usually save money by combining the two types of survey, provided the lender accepts the surveyor's valuation. If you have any particular concerns point these out to the surveyor and ask for a more detailed inspection. Put your request in writing, so if a fault appears after you have moved in you can claim redress from the surveyor.

New homes

If you are buying a new property or a recently-built home it will probably be covered by a 10-year warranty. These are issued when homes are first built, but are transferred to new owners if the house is sold within the warranty period.

There are two types of warranty: The National House Building Council (NHBC) and The Zurich Municipal warranty.

If you are buying a newer home you may feel that you can dispense with a survey. However, one may still be advisable if the warranty is nearing its end. The NHBC 'Buildmark' cover will pay for the cost of any work not properly completed by the builder within the first two years. After that it won't pay for anything that was or could have been reported to the builder.

9 Contracts: From Draft to Exchange and Completion

Preparing to Exchange Contracts

While your solicitor/conveyancer is starting to make the checks outlined earlier, the vendor's solicitor will be preparing a draft contract. Most of the checks that your side needs to make will be found in this draft contract, which will include information about:

- the address of the property

- the name of the vendor/buyer

- the purchase price

- a summary of the title deeds or the registered details

Your solicitor/conveyancer will then make any further enquiries that are necessary.

> **Warning:** It is essential that you receive a copy of the draft contract and read it carefully. The solicitors may be unaware that you have agreed with the vendor that certain repairs will be completed before exchange of contracts or that certain items (such as carpets and curtains) are included in the sale. You must make sure that this information is written into the contract. Just because you have a verbal agreement does not mean the vendor will stick to his or her word.

Once your solicitor/conveyancer has finalized all the checks and both of you are satisfied that the contract covers all the necessary points, a final contract will be drawn up. This process can take some time, particularly if both sides amend the contract several times. To speed up and simplify conveyancing the Law Society introduced a scheme known as the 'Transaction Protocol'. Many solicitors use this. Under the scheme the seller's solicitor provides a package of information including:

▌ a copy of the draft contract

▌ copies of entries on the Land Register (or title deeds if unregistered)

▌ a list of answers to preliminary enquiries; this property information form will answer many of the questions your solicitor/conveyancer will need to ask

▌ a pre-printed form detailing which fixtures, fittings and contents are to be included in the sale

▌ the local authority and other searches (you will pay for these searches, but they will have already been done, eliminating any delays while local authorities conduct the search)

It is this point in the homebuying process that is the most stressful. Not only will you now face several potential problems, but if things go wrong you could end up out of pocket.

Gazumping

It is at this point that you are most vulnerable to gazumping – losing the property because another purchaser has offered a higher price or is ready to exchange contracts before you.

If you are gazumped you will lose any legal and survey/valuation fees you have already paid or incurred. And you must be prepared for this to happen to you – some unlucky buyers see three or four sales fall through in this way.

Reform of the Housebuying Process

The government plans to change the entire homebuying process to reduce the problem of gazumping.

Under government proposals it will be up to the seller – not the buyer – to pay for the cost of most of the basic information such as local authority searches and compiling information regarding leases and deeds.

This will speed up the homebuying process, making it harder for gazumpers. After all, if the sale proceeds in a matter of a few weeks rather than months there is less scope for another buyer to come along and offer a higher price.

The government hopes that the average time it takes to buy a home – the time from when an offer is made and accepted to completion – will be reduced significantly from the current average of 12 weeks to 4 weeks.

The so-called 'seller's pack' will cost around £500 and will include a basic survey, local authority search, draft contract, title deeds and a form answering common legal queries. The advantage is that only one buyer has to pay for all these costs rather than several if there are a number of unsuccessful attempts to buy the property.

Scotland

In Scotland houses are bought and sold by tender. When vendors put their home on the market, interested buyers put in bids and the highest bid is accepted. Once that happens it becomes a legally binding contract.

The advantage of this system is that gazumping does not happen. The disadvantage is that you may pay for a survey (or several surveys on various properties) and then be outbid several times.

Chains are also avoided. Sellers give themselves enough time to find a new home by stating an entry date, when the new owner can move in. However, there can be drawbacks. Those moving home often have to find bridging finance to cover two mortgages as they may have to move in to their new home before selling their existing one, or they may be forced to live in temporary accommodation if they have sold their property but have not found a new one.

Sales are usually handled by solicitors who often act as an agent to the seller as well as doing the conveyancing.

Contract Races

If a vendor is in a particular hurry to sell, he or she may accept offers from two or more buyers. Whoever is ready to exchange contracts first will then get the property. The other bidders, however, will have paid for legal, surveying and other fees and these costs – and the stress involved – will be for nothing.

Although it is better to avoid a contract race wherever possible, you may not know that you are involved in one. Sometimes buyers only find out that another purchaser is in the race by accident or – even worse – when it is too late and the property has been sold to someone else.

Chains

A chain is when a buyer has first to sell his or her existing property (property 'A') and in turn the buyer of property 'A' must sell their home (property 'B') to someone else who may also need to sell their property (property 'C'). There can often be three or four homes exchanging on one day to complete a chain. As a first-time buyer you will not have to worry about selling your existing home, but if you are caught up in a chain you must be prepared for delays and problems if other sales in the property chain fall through or are delayed.

If you are very keen to buy a particular property make sure you exchange contracts as soon as possible but leave the completion date open. That way you know the sale will not fall through and the vendor cannot keep the property on the market hoping for a higher price in a few weeks' (or even months') time.

Exchange of Contracts

It may have taken you months of searching for properties, being outbid and even being gazumped to get to this point. Only now can you start to relax a little as once you exchange contracts, you can be relatively sure that the property is yours.

Exchange of contracts simply means that both the buyer and the vendor sign identical documents, committing them to the sale, and then swap them over.

Once you have done this you have entered into a legally binding agreement from which neither side can withdraw.

The Deposit

Just before contracts are exchanged you will need to hand over a non-refundable deposit, which is usually 10 per cent of the purchase price, although it can be lower (5 per cent) by mutual agreement.

Remember, if for some reason you have to pull out of the sale you will lose this deposit and may be sued for breach of contract.

Your mortgage lender will not advance the home loan until completion (the date that you move in, which is usually two to four weeks after you have exchanged contracts). If you have difficulty in raising the deposit – this will be if your mortgage is for more than 90 per cent of the property value – ask your mortgage lender for advice. If you qualify for a mortgage you should be able to get a short-term loan or bridging finance.

Checks before Signing

Most of the final checks will be undertaken by your solicitor/conveyancer. They include:

▌ confirming that mortgage finance is agreed in writing, all lending conditions have been met and the lender will be able to advance the required home loan on the completion date

▌ checking that both the buyer and mortgage lender have no problems with the results of the survey/valuation and the preliminary enquiries and local searches

▌ agreeing a completion date – the date when ownership will be transferred to the buyer

▌ checking that all terms are agreed between the buyer and seller

Signing the Contract

Do not get caught up in the excitement and forget to question anything on the contract you do not understand or ask why a particular point has not been covered.

This is your last chance to make sure that you understand everything and are happy with the agreement. Remember, if you have any doubts – for instance, you do not think you can live by a dual carriageway after all – you can still pull out of the sale. It may be better to lose the surveying and legal fees than to buy a home that you do not really want to live in.

From Exchange to Completion

You will now have just two to four weeks to prepare your move (although this can be longer if you have agreed a later date with the vendor).

Checklist – What You Need To Do Now

▌ arrange for buildings and contents insurance (if you have not already agreed to buy this from your lender) to come into force on the date you move in

▌ book a removal van

▌ inform the following that you intend to move on a certain date:

- gas board – and ask for a meter reading on your existing home and new home
- telephone company – to ensure you are connected at your new address and disconnected at your old address
- electricity company – again to ensure that meters are read
- your bank
- your employer

▌ finally confirm the date you will move out of your current accommodation

▌ arrange to register with a new doctor and dentist

▌ send out change of address cards

▌ ensure your mortgage finance is still in place

▌ ensure life cover is in force (it is advisable to have this put 'on risk' on the date you exchange contracts to cover the mortgage debt if the worst happens before you complete on the property purchase)

▌ check that all your other financing (for instance to pay for legal fees and removal costs) is in place

▌ arrange time off from work to move

The Transfer Document

While you are frantically trying to arrange your move, your solicitor/conveyancer will be arranging the transfer document. If the property is already registered with the Land Registry the document is called The Transfer. If it is not, a different form of conveyance form will be used. Both the vendor and buyer must usually sign The Transfer.

Your solicitor/conveyancer will also check that the mortgage documents are in order, will conduct any final searches and enquiries –

for instance whether any further charges have been registered against the property – and will send a 'Requisition on Title' form to the vendor's solicitor/conveyancer.

Completion: the Costs

Before you can finally complete the purchase you will have to start writing out cheques to pay for some of the more expensive bills involved in homebuying. These include:

▌ stamp duty

▌ Land Registry fees

▌ solicitors'/conveyancing fees (either before or on completion)

You should also check the vendor has completed any works agreed in the contract.

Mortgage finance will usually be paid over by CHAPS (clearing house automated payment system) electronic transfer at mid-day on the date of completion. You will be charged for this transfer.

Completion Day

Completion is usually at mid-day. By this time:

▌ the balance of the price of the house (the purchase price less the deposit) should be transferred to the vendor

▌ the seller's deeds will be handed to your solicitor/conveyancer and any outstanding mortgages on the property paid off

Once this has been done the seller must move out – giving you vacant possession – and the keys will be handed over.

> **Warning:** There can sometimes be delays on completion day and as such you may find that your removal van is sitting outside your new home for a few hours while the vendor waits for confirmation from his or her solicitor/conveyancer that full funds to purchase the property have been transferred.

While you are preparing to unpack, your solicitor should tie up any loose ends, including:

- notifying your lender, life insurance company and the freeholder (if the property is leasehold) that completion has taken place

- registering the change of ownership at the Land Registry and, once this is done, forwarding deeds to your mortgage lender

- paying the stamp duty

Your solicitor/conveyancer will also send you a completion statement breaking down the costs and – if you have not paid this already – you will be sent the final bill for conveyancing.

10 Moving In

Completion is usually on a Friday – often the last Friday of the month. As a result you should be prepared for removal firms or removal vans to be fully booked, for heavy traffic and – if anything goes wrong – remember, you will have to wait until Monday to sort it out.

As this is your first home purchase, you may not be prepared for the problems involved in moving. To minimize these, you should bear the following in mind:

▌ Book your rented removal van/removal firm in plenty of time. Shop around for the best deal and, if you are paying someone to move your belongings for you, check that they are reputable and have adequate insurance to cover any loss or damage to your belongings.

▌ Be prepared for the gas board, electricity company and telephone company to turn up at any time. You may be stuck in a traffic jam a mile away and miss your appointment. To err on the safe side, ask a friend or relative to wait by your new home to ensure that the utility company can gain access or will wait a few minutes for you to arrive with the keys.

▌ The same applies to deliveries. If you are expecting a new cooker, fridge or bed to be delivered, make sure you agree a set time, preferably later in the afternoon to allow for any delays. Ring the delivery firm earlier in the day to check the time of delivery. Remember, if something goes wrong you may have to wait until Monday to sort it out

▌ Be prepared for the vendor to leave the property:
  - in a mess
  - without any lightbulbs (yes some sellers do take them away)
  - without any services – they may have asked for these to be disconnected
  - littered with rubbish or unwanted furniture

To reduce the stress and give yourself more time to move, arrange to move out of your existing accommodation a few days or even a week after moving into your new home. That way you will have plenty of time to clean the new property, redecorate, arrange for carpets to be laid and equipment delivered before moving in your belongings.

One of the many things you may have forgotten to check when you viewed the property is whether it will be easy to move your furniture in – a potential removal problem.

Hiring a Van

As a first-time buyer you may not have much furniture, and as such can save money by making the move yourself.

▌ When comparing costs, make sure you include the cost of insurance.

▌ Don't try to cut costs by not buying insurance or not buying adequate insurance.

▌ You will generally need to have a clean driving licence to hire a van and will usually have to pay by credit card.

▌ Check that your driving licence allows you to drive the size of van required and that you meet the hire company's conditions. For instance, they may require that you have been driving for at least three years. Imagine booking a van, only to find on the day of moving you are not allowed to drive it.

▌ Don't book a van that is too large – you may find it difficult to drive and hard to park.

▌ Ask if the van has a lift to help you to load and unload.

▌ Find out if you can hire boxes or tea chests to store or pack your belongings.

▌ Ask friends to help you – even if you only have a few belongings you will probably find that they take longer to move than you think.

▌ Read the terms and conditions of your rental agreement carefully to make sure you meet all the conditions – such as returning the van by a particular time.

Hiring a Removal Firm

▌ Make sure you pick a reputable firm. You don't want to find that on the day of your move they fail to turn up, supply the wrong size van or are late. Contact the British Association of Removers (020 8861 3331) for a list of three local firms who are members of the association and for free leaflets on moving (you will need to send an sae to 3 Churchill Court, 58 Station Road, North Harrow, Middlesex, HA2 7SA).

▌ Get quotes/estimates from at least two firms. The estimator should inspect your property to get a more accurate idea of your needs and the costs involved.

▌ Check if you are to be charged on an hourly rate, a half day rate or whole day rate and find out how much you will be charged if the move takes longer than estimated.

▌ Find out how much insurance cover the removal firm has bought. Often the maximum pay-out in the event of damage or loss is very small and the terms and conditions for making a claim are restrictive.

▌ To cut costs you can consider:
  - packing your own belongings in boxes/crates supplied by the removal firm
  - packing your own breakables including crockery and glass (but if you fail to do this as carefully as the professionals you could find that the costs of replacing items outweigh the savings)
  - unpacking your own belongings
  - hiring your own boxes/crates

▌ When booking your removal firm you will probably have to confirm the date and time of your move. Ask if you have to pay a cancellation fee if, for some reason, the move does not go ahead or the date of the move is changed.

▌ Make sure you have put your agreement in writing. The removal firm will probably have a standard contract, but you may want to write an additional letter confirming: the number of removal men, how many packing boxes will be supplied and how much you will be charged if the move takes longer than agreed.

What You Will Need to Help You Move

As discussed earlier, you may find that your new home needs a thorough clean on the day you move in. You will also have to leave your existing home in good condition. Useful tips include:

▌ Make sure you keep cleaning materials separate. You will need a vacuum cleaner, broom, dustpan and brush, rubbish sacks and cleaning materials.

▌ Keep anything you need on the first night in a separate bag – for instance, your toothbrush, a kettle and some teabags and milk, some lightbulbs and candles (just in case the electricity is not connected in time), and some change for the phone box (in case the phone is not connected).

▮ Make sure you keep any necessary paperwork within easy reach – your removal contract, any correspondence from the gas/electricity/telephone company and a list of telephone numbers including those for your solicitor/conveyancer, mortgage lender, estate agent and removal firm.

What You Need to Leave Behind

Make sure you have left or handed over to the new occupant:

▮ all the keys – including those for cupboards and windows

▮ a forwarding address

What You Must Check You Have Been Given

When you arrive at the new property either the estate agent or vendor will hand you over a set of keys to the property, or you will have to go to the estate agent's office to collect these.

Make sure you have been handed all sets of keys and also check the vendor has handed over or left behind:

▮ copies of all instruction leaflets (for instance, for the boiler)

▮ copies of any guarantees

▮ a forwarding address

What You Must Do Now

Although unpacking may be high on your list of priorities, there are other things you must do urgently.

▮ Check nothing has been broken or damaged in the move. If you used a removal firm make sure that you inform the removal firm of any damage as soon as possible. Notify the removal firm in writing within the time limit (see your contract for how to make a claim).

▌ Make sure your insurance policy on your new home is in force.

▌ Check that you meet the terms of your insurance policy – that door and window locks are of the required standard.

▌ Arrange for locks on the outer doors to be changed – you do not know who could have a copy of these.

▌ Keep all documents relating to the move in a safe place in case you need to refer to them at a later date.

£ CASH TIP £

If you have moved because your firm has relocated you, and your company has paid your relocation expenses, you will usually be able to receive the first £8000 of these removal costs free of tax.

---

11 Buildings and Contents Insurance

As discussed earlier, it is essential that you do have insurance in place from the date that you move into your new property. It is advisable to keep any insurance policies on your existing home in place for a few extra days after the move, to protect your belongings should the move take longer than expected.

Buildings and contents insurance are generally bought as a package. However, there is nothing to stop you from shopping around and buying them separately. But be aware that should you make a claim, you will have to deal with two insurance companies and there may be problems in agreeing which insurer covers what. Some first-time buyers decide that as contents insurance can be very expensive (particularly in an inner-city area) they will not bother to insure their furniture and belongings. This is usually a false economy. Even if you feel you can afford to replace your old TV and video should they be stolen, could you still afford to be without insurance should your home burn down or flood and you must replace **everything**?

You will not be able to dispense with buildings insurance as this will be a requirement of your mortgage unless you are buying a leasehold flat, in which case check the freeholder has got it. You will have to prove you have cover if you do not buy this insurance from your lender.

Warning: Even if you have arranged insurance you must still check that the policy has come into force. If your new home burns down on the day you move in, and you have no cover, you will be left homeless and in severe financial difficulties.

> **Tip:** It is usually very easy to cut the average £300 a year insurance bill by shopping around.

When to Buy it

Buildings insurance should be arranged *before* you move into a property. Cover may have to begin from the date of exchange of contracts – not the date of completion or the date when you plan to move into the property.

Under the terms of the TransAction protocol (a legal system for conveyancing), insurance should remain the responsibility of the vendor until completion, so you may be able to delay insuring the property until then. Your solicitor should be able to advise you when you should start cover. If you are buying a new home from a developer, insurance normally remains the responsibility of the builder until completion.

Although you will not have moved into the property, insurance before completion is essential if the property is no longer at the seller's risk. It will cover you for any burst pipes, damage because of storms or theft or fire, from the day you exchange to the day you move in.

Contents insurance does not need to be in place until the day you move in. If you are moving over several days make sure your existing policy remains in force to cover your belongings in your old home until you have finally moved out.

If you have purchased a flat, the buildings insurance will generally be included as part of your service charges. Your solicitor should check that cover is in place. You may have to request a more detailed document showing what the policy covers and excludes.

When you buy a property your solicitor should ensure that buildings insurance is in place.

Who Sells it

Your Mortgage Lender

Your bank or building society may require that you take out buildings and contents insurance as a condition of the mortgage, so you may not be able to shop around for a better deal. After pressure from the Office of Fair Trading, lenders are only allowed to impose this condition if the loan itself is a special offer, such as a discount or fixed rate mortgage.

Even if insurance is not compulsory, your lender may still encourage you to take out insurance with an insurance company it is tied to or owns.

One recent survey found that homeowners who buy their buildings and contents insurance through their mortgage lender are paying up to 78 per cent more than they need to. Research by Zurich Insurance put this figure at an average of £73 a year. If you want to switch to a cheaper alternative you will probably be charged for administration – usually £25. But it may still be worth shopping around as you could easily save £100 a year and often your new insurer will refund the £25 administration fee.

The advantage of buying insurance from your lender is that it will often make paying your premiums easier. Lenders often pay the first premium (but they will deduct this from your mortgage advance) to ensure that cover is in place. Some building societies add the insurance premiums to your monthly mortgage repayments to spread the cost over the year.

Direct Insurance Companies

These sell insurance over the telephone and can be cheaper. To get the best insurance deals you have to be a low 'risk'. This means that if you are buying a property in an area which has a high crime rate or a high risk of subsidence you will pay more or may find that you cannot get cover. Likewise, the insurer will expect that you have a high level of security as a minimum requirement. Most direct insurers require British Standard five-lever door locks and window locks and will not meet your claims if you fail to use these (for instance, your policy may require that all windows bar the one in the bedroom must be locked at night).

> **Warning:** If you buy insurance over the telephone you will not see the policy terms and conditions in advance and may unwittingly fail to disclose 'material facts' – such as past insurance claims – which could invalidate your policy. Once you have received the policy contract you should read it thoroughly to make sure you meet the terms and conditions and comply with all security requirements. If you don't, you could find that any future claims are rejected. You should also read the policy wording to check what is actually covered.

Insurance Brokers

An insurance broker will aim to find you the cheapest policy to meet your needs. As different insurance companies have different risk ratings for each postcode area, you could find that one charges much more to insure your property than another. The broker will also be able to take special factors into account (for instance, selecting an insurer that gives discounts to those with extra household security or ones that specialize in giving lower amounts of cover).

£ CASH TIP £

If you are a teacher, member of a trade union or a professional body you may find that certain insurance companies offer you cheap insurance. An insurance broker should be able to advise you.

What the Policy Covers

Buildings

The fabric of your home – bricks and mortar, windows, roof, floors and anything that is a fixture or fitting such as your kitchen units, built-in wardrobes and doors. So while the floorboards are covered under buildings insurance, the carpets are not.

Contents

Anything that is not a fixture, including personal belongings, curtains, carpets, furniture and clothes. Some contents policies also cover personal belongings while they are outside the home. Others have a maximum limit on the value of individual items, so if you have any expensive items of jewellery or photographic equipment these may have to be insured separately or for an additional premium. If you own a bicycle you will normally have to pay an additional premium to insure it.

At the more expensive end of the spectrum a policy can also cover:

▌ accidental damage to your contents (and should be considered for buildings as it will cover a foot through the ceiling while you are in the loft)

▌ all risks, which covers belongings, including cash, taken out of the home.

Legal Protection Cover

This pays for legal advice and will help you deal with consumer, employment or contractual disputes and is offered by many insurers as an addition to home or motor insurance. Check what is covered and how much it costs. If you already have this cover as part of membership of a trade union or professional body, make sure you do not buy two lots of cover.

£ CASH TIP £

Most insurers also offer a 24-hour household emergency service. Make sure that this is free and check what it covers. Look for one that puts you in touch with qualified tradesmen who can fix a broken pipe or repair a storm damaged roof for a reasonable price and quickly and efficiently.

How Much Cover?

Buildings

The amount you are insured for is the cost of rebuilding *not* the market valuation. Rebuild valuations are normally lower than the price you actually pay for the property.

The rebuild cost is usually determined at the time of purchase and then rises in line with inflation in building costs. Either the building society valuer or your surveyor will provide the figure for the amount of cover you should buy.

Some policies avoid the problem of calculating an exact rebuild value by insuring the property on the basis of the number of rooms or bedrooms.

If you have bought a flat you should not have to worry about the level of cover as this should be arranged by the freeholder. Your solicitor will check that adequate cover is in place.

Warning: If, after you move into your property, you plan major renovations or alterations you could find that this affects the rebuild value of your property. Make sure you increase your buildings cover accordingly.

Contents

As a first-time buyer, the value of your contents may be very low. Some insurers will have a minimum amount that they will insure (say £10,000) and you may feel that you do not need this level of cover. However, the value of contents can quickly mount up once you take into account the cost of replacing your entire record collection or the contents of your wardrobe.

Before taking out cover you should make a list of all your contents and the cost of replacing them. Keep this in a safe place along with any receipts. And update the list regularly. In the event of a total loss (a flood or fire) this list will help support your claim. When making a list of your contents use the following checklist:

- furniture – beds, sofas, chairs, tables, bookshelves, cupboards and wardrobes (not fitted)

- soft furnishings – curtains, carpets, cushions

- linen, etc – bed linen, duvets, blankets, pillows

- lamps/light fittings – lamps, light fittings, lightbulbs

- electrical items – TV, video, stereo, radio/alarm clock, CD player, computer, printer, etc

- clothing – include everything from underwear and shoes to coats and boots

- kitchen contents – pots, pans, food, freezer contents, kettle, toaster, spices, plates, cutlery, etc

- bathroom contents – toiletries and towels

- personal belongings – books, records, CDs, videos, photographs/picture frames, cameras, musical equipment, paintings/posters, etc

Take expert advice when buying your first home.

Buying your first home is very exciting but finding a suitable mortgage can be a daunting prospect. With so many mortgage loans on offer from so many different lenders, just how do you find one to suit you?

CGU, one of the UK's leading financial services companies can help. As part of our Mortgage Service CGU are committed to finding a mortgage to match your individual needs.

This no obligation service is provided by our highly trained, salaried financial consultants who have access to an array of mortgage lenders. If you went to a Building Society or Bank you would receive advice only on the mortgage loans offered by that

Society or Bank. The CGU mortgage service saves you time and worry.

You don't even need to be buying your home through CGU's estate agency chain - the Mortgage Service is available to everyone even if you are buying your home through another estate agency or simply want to remortgage for a better deal, the Mortgage Service is at your disposal.

Contacting a CGU financial consultant is easy too – simply telephone **0800 917 3900** quoting reference 1846/01 to find out where your nearest one is based.

Buying a new home should be exciting and by getting CGU to help perhaps the only thing you will have to worry about is the colour of that bathroom.

CGU financial consultants can help you throughout the whole homebuying process by

- **finding a mortgage that's right for you**

- **advising on methods of mortgage repayment**

- **selecting a solicitor and surveyor**

- **advising on buildings and contents insurance.**

YOUR HOME IS AT RISK IF YOU DO NOT KEEP UP REPAYMENTS ON A MORTGAGE OR OTHER LOAN SECURED ON IT

CGU Life Services Limited
Registered in England No. 2403746
2 Rougier Street York YO90 1UU
Regulated by the Personal Investment Authority.

You'll be moved

when we find the

right mortgage lender for you

For further details
call free on 0800 917 3900
quoting reference 1846/01

CGU

How to value contents

Most policies pay for you to replace items if they are stolen, damaged or destroyed. So you will need to find the cost of buying these items at today's prices. The easiest way to value items is to keep receipts or alternatively check out the prices in your local high street.

Bedroom rated policies

Some insurers do not cover you for an exact amount, but base the insurance on the number of bedrooms (or rooms) in the property. If the value of the contents in your property is low, you may be better off insuring for an exact amount.

> **Warning:** If you do not insure your property or its contents for the full value – either initially or because you have not increased your cover following extensive improvements or increases in the value of your contents – your insurer will probably not meet your claim in full.

For further information

The Association of British Insurers (020 7600 3333) produces a free leaflet, *Buildings Insurance for Home Owners*, to help you check that you have the right amount of cover.

What You are Insured Against

Buildings

Most policies cover you against theft, fire, storms (but not damage to fences or hedges), flood and subsidence. You should also be covered against vandalism or malicious acts and theft or attempted theft and damage caused by water (burst pipes) or oil leaking from a heating installation or domestic appliance. Accidental damage to glass in windows and doors, fixed ceramic hobs and fixed sanitary ware should also be covered. Cover also includes insurance against riot, civil commotion, labour or political disturbance and damage caused by collision with the building (for instance a lorry driving into your home). If the worst happens and you have to move out of your home while it is being repaired, the cost of alternative accommodation will also be met.

Exclusions

The policy will not cover you for theft or vandalism by a guest or tenant or any theft, damage from burst pipes or vandalism if the home has been unoccupied for more than 30 consecutive days. Subsidence caused by coastal or river erosion is also excluded as is any damage caused to patios, garden walls, footpaths and terraces by subsidence.

Contents

As above, you are covered against damage caused by fire, lightning, explosions, smoke, theft, storms, floods, vandalism and burst pipes, and cover usually includes the contents of your garden, contents while they are temporarily taken out of the home, damage to locks and accidental damage to certain items (accidental damage cover usually costs extra).

Exclusions

You will not generally be covered if you fail to take care of your property and do not ensure adequate security. There is usually a limit on the value of individual items, so expensive items must either be insured separately or for an additional premium. If you leave your home empty for more than 30 consecutive days you may also no longer be covered. Damage or theft by a paying guest or tenant is also not covered. And accidental damage may not cover records, discs, video tapes or cassettes. If your property has suffered from subsidence in the past, cover against this may be excluded.

> **Warning:** If you are planning to rent out a room to help pay your mortgage you should tell your insurer. Otherwise, if any damage is caused by a tenant; he or she steals any of your belongings or leaves the door unlocked, your insurance claim will probably be rejected.

How Much Does it Cost?

Buildings

Cover starts at about £1.30 for every £1000 insured, but can rise to as much as £4 per £1000. So on a property with a rebuild value of £50,000 you could pay between £65 and £200. However, in some cases you may have to pay more (for instance if you are buying a thatched property). Average premiums are £128.04, although they can be cut to £89.51 if you shop around, according to the AA's insurance premium index for the second quarter of 1999.

Contents

This can vary from under £100 to almost £1000, depending on the level of cover and how good a risk you are perceived to be by the insurer. Average premiums are £103.63 but can drop to £69.24 if you shop around.

£ CASH TIP £

Some insurance companies offer a discount if you buy more than one policy. So if you buy both your buildings and contents insurance from the same company, you may be able to reduce the costs of insurance significantly.

Low-cost Contents Insurance

One way to cut costs is to opt for an insurance policy that does not replace items that are stolen or destroyed, but only gives you the second-hand value. These are not generally a good idea. If your property burnt to the ground and you had to replace everything you own you would be left out of pocket. You will be better off with 'new for old' which gives you the replacement value.

However, if you live in a high risk area where insurance premiums are high and most of your furniture is second hand or very cheap, you can consider this type of policy if your budget is very tight and this is the only insurance you can afford.

What Affects the Cost of Insurance?

In addition to the level of cover and the type of policy, you will pay more if you have a greater risk of making a claim.

Most insurance policies are determined by postcode. So if you live in an inner-city area that has a high number of burglaries, or are buying a property in a region that is more prone to subsidence, you will pay more. And if you have made a claim in the recent past, you may also be charged more.

However, you can reduce the risks and therefore the costs of insurance. The following usually enable householders to claim a discount on their premiums:

▪ Increase your home's security devices – discounts for approved door and window locks are around 5 per cent as for an approved burglar alarm (you will probably be required to have an annual maintenance contract for this).

▪ Join (or set up) a neighbourhood watch scheme.

▪ In some cases, double glazing is also classed as a burglar deterrent.

▌ Do you have someone at home all day? This reduces the risks of burglary and therefore your insurance premiums.

▌ Some insurers offer discounts if you install a smoke alarm.

Warning: Some insurers require a minimum level of security – five-lever mortice locks on the front door and window locks – before they will provide you with cover.

The Policy Excess

This is the amount which you pay towards any insurance claim. So if you make a subsidence claim you may have to pay the first £500 or £2000 of the costs. For a contents claim you may have to pay the first £50 of any claim.

The higher the excess, the lower the premiums. Some insurers allow you to increase the excess to reduce the insurance costs.

Reading the Small Print

It is essential that you read the terms of your policy thoroughly, if only to ensure that you are not breaching any of the requirements or paying for any insurance cover that you do not need.

For instance, you may not realize that the expensive accidental damage cover you have bought does not cover damage caused by pets. Or the policy may require that the home is occupied solely by 'the policyholder, spouse or partner'. If you work from home, your business equipment may not be covered. If you qualify for a discount because you have a burglar alarm, you may find your claim is refused because you failed to turn it on.

Problems Making a Claim

A recent *Which?* survey found that one in seven people had their claim down-valued by their insurer. So you should be aware of the circumstances in which a claim will be reduced. Often it is the fault of the householder who has failed to meet the policy terms and conditions.

Why a Claim May Be Reduced

Wear and tear

Most policies pay out sufficient to replace your damaged or stolen goods with new items. These are known as 'new for old' policies. However, in some cases the insurer may make a deduction for 'wear and tear', and only give you the second-hand value. This can sometimes be the case when you claim for items such as bed linen.

You have not met the policy terms and conditions

If your policy requires that you fit five-bar mortice locks on your door and you fail to use these, you could find that they are reluctant to meet your burglary claim. Likewise if you fail to lock your bicycle and it is stolen, you have failed to meet the policy's conditions.

You do not have sufficient cover

If you have insured your building for only 80 per cent of its rebuilding value you cannot expect the insurance company to pay for all the rebuilding costs. Contents insurance claims can also be scaled down in this way.

Repair rather than replacement

In some cases the insurance company may insist that damaged items are repaired rather than replaced. In this case, make sure that the repairers return the item to its original state and follow the procedures for getting quotes from repair firms or else the insurer may claim the costs are too high.

Insurance Investigations

In some cases – particularly if you are making a large or unusual claim – the insurance company will send round a loss adjuster to examine your insurance claim. This does not mean that the insurance company thinks your claim is fraudulent. However, the loss adjuster will check that your claim is genuine, that you have met the terms and conditions of your insurance policy and that you are claiming a reasonable amount.

You do not pay the loss adjuster's fees – these are met by the insurance company.

Even if the adjuster reduces the size of the claim, you can dispute this if you think this is unfair. To ensure you receive the maximum insurance payout (particularly for major claims) you can employ a loss assessor.

Switching Insurers

If you are in an area that is at risk from subsidence, you may have a problem should you need to claim after you have switched insurers. Your new insurance company may claim that some of the damage was caused before you switched policies. However, a recent agreement among insurers should mean that this is now less of a problem.

Protecting Your Property

Insurance is there to protect you should the worst happen. However, it is far better to avoid making a claim. Take the following precautions:

▌ Install smoke alarms, and check that they are working properly on a regular basis.

▌ Mark your postcode on your property with an indelible/invisible-ink pen.

▌ Do not overload electrical sockets, get your wiring checked and ensure all appliances are correctly fused.

▌ Cut back hedges and foliage near to the property – burglars are more likely to target your property if they know they will not be seen.

▌ Install outside lights that are triggered when anyone approaches the property.

▌ If you are ever away from home cancel milk/paper deliveries. An obviously empty house is an open invitation to burglars.

▌ Ask your local crime prevention officer (ask at your local police station) to help you minimize the risks of burglary.

▌ Don't leave any items such as gardening equipment unlocked – they may be stolen or used by a burglar to help gain access to the property.

▌ Lag pipes in the attic and the water tank to minimize the risk of burst pipes and flooding.

▌ Switch off all electrical items that are on 'standby', such as your TV, when leaving the property (this will also cut your electricity bill).

12 Problems With Your New Home

Once you have started to settle in, you may find that the central heating does not work properly or that the floorboards are rotten, but this was not pointed out on your survey.

As a result you may want to complain to the vendor or your surveyor and seek compensation. However, you will probably find it difficult and expensive.

Complaints You May Have Against the Vendor

▌ Failing to leave behind items included in the contract.

▌ Failing to undertake repairs included in the contract.

▌ Wrongfully declaring that items – such as the central heating system, damp course or wiring – were under guarantee.

In these cases, you can ask your solicitor to make a claim against the vendor for, say, the return of an item and the cost of re-installing it. However, once you are involved in the legal process it can be costly and time consuming. If you have a legal expenses policy you will probably be able to pursue your case for free. The alternative is to take the vendor to the Small Claims Court.

However, there are some complaints that you cannot pursue. Remember, the golden rule of homebuying is *caveat emptor* or buyer beware. For example:

▌ The central heating does not work – the vendor only needs to state that the property has central heating, it is up to you to check that it works (you should have asked your surveyor to check or employed a gas engineer to do this for you).

▌ The vendor has removed the mirrors that seemed to be part of the fireplace or the Welsh dresser that appeared to be part of the fitted kitchen. Disputes about what is a fixture and fitting and what is not are not uncommon. You will find it hard to pursue your complaint unless the items were specifically mentioned in the list of what was included and excluded in the sale.

Complaints You May Have Against the Estate Agent

You will only have a case if the problem is the result of false information. You may then be able to claim against the estate agent under the Property Misdescriptions Act. However, as your solicitor should have made all the relevant checks you should have already found out that the property was not as described in the estate agent's particulars. If you have signed a contract that includes the corrected information you may find that your case is very weak.

For instance, if the estate agent's particulars state the property has fitted wardrobes but these are removed by the vendor, and this fact was pointed out in the contract, you will have no case as you had agreed to this when you signed the contract.

Complaints You May Have Against the Surveyor

You may feel that your surveyor should have pointed out certain defects in his or her report. For instance:

▌ you move in and find that the roof is leaking

▌ when you pull up the old carpets you find the floorboards are rotten

▌ when clearing out under the stairs you find that there is damp

▌ fuses keep blowing and you employ an electrician who tells you the wiring is dangerous

You may think that you have a good case against your surveyor, but if you read your survey report you may find otherwise. The surveyor may have written 'unable to inspect floorboards as property had fitted carpets' or 'roof not inspected as could not get access'. Unless you specifically asked the surveyor to check these points you may find you have no case.

Even if you do, you will then have to prove that the surveyor was negligent. This does not just mean that he or she made a mistake. You will have to prove that this mistake was 'gross' and that the defect should have been one that a skilled professional ought to have spotted.

When it comes to seeking redress, you can use the Royal Institution of Chartered Surveyors' arbitration service. For information contact:

The RICS
12 Great George Street
London
SW1P 3AD

020 7222 7000

The scheme, which costs £250 plus VAT, is legally binding. So if you do not agree with the decision, hard luck. You cannot then sue your surveyor. The more costly alternative is taking your surveyor to court. This will not only be expensive and time consuming but, even if you do win, you will only be compensated for any reduction in value of the property as a result of the defect.

So a new roof may cost you £10,000, but if it had been known the roof was in poor repair the value of the property would only be reduced by £2000. Thus you will only get £2000 compensation and still be £8000 out of pocket. If you lose your case you will have to pay the surveyor's legal costs and you will need to employ experts – other surveyors, etc – to prove your case. The alternative is to reduce the amount of compensation you are seeking and take your case to the Small Claims Court.

Complaints You May Have Against Your Lender

If your lender has left you out of pocket by changing the terms of the mortgage at the last minute, or by making an administrative error that caused delays and extra costs, you should initially complain to the complaints department at the head office. As a last resort, you can take your case to either the:

Building Society Ombudsman
Millbank Tower
Millbank
London
SW1P 4XS

020 7931 0044

or

The Banking Ombudsman
70 Gray's Inn Road
London
WC1X 8NB

020 7404 9944

Complaints You May Have Against Your Solicitor/Conveyancer

If you have received a poor quality or slow service, but did not lose out financially as a result, you may be able to complain to:

The Office for the Supervision of Solicitors
Victoria Court
8 Dormer Place
Leamington Spa
Warwickshire
CV32 5AE

01926 820082

or

The Council for Licensed Conveyancers
16 Glebe Road
Chelmsford
Essex
CM1 1QG

01245 349599

Under the Office for the Supervision of Solicitors scheme you can
receive compensation or a refund of fees up to £1000. If you are
seeking financial compensation – for instance the solicitor fails to
spot a major problem such as a restriction on the lease that means
the flat is worth less than you paid for it – you can take your complaint to:

The Legal Services Ombudsman
22 Oxford Court
Oxford Street
Manchester
M2 3WQ

0161 236 9532

As a last resort you may want to make a claim against your solicitor's or conveyancer's negligence insurance. The Law Society has a
panel of solicitors who will take on cases against other solicitors.
Apply to:

The Law Society
113 Chancery Lane
London
WC2A 1PL

020 7242 1222

Complaints You May Have Against a House Builder

As discussed earlier in this book, even when moving into a new property you should expect problems. Few new homes are sold without some needing some minor repairs, even if these are only adjusting a door fitting or replacing a chipped tile.

Follow the claim procedure under your NHBC or other guarantee and make sure you put all complaints in writing.

13 Repairs, Renovations and Home Improvements

Even if you are moving into a brand new home, you will find that there is a certain amount of work to be done. This may only involve putting up shelves, curtains and light fittings, but you will still find that the costs quickly mount up.

Remember your home is your home – not just an investment. In many cases you may find that the costs of repairs and renovations are not recouped on sale, but you are still prepared to pay for them as they will enhance your enjoyment of the property.

But you should also be aware that in some cases your 'improvements' can actually reduce the value of your property. So before you start using your electric drill or employing a builder to knock down a wall or remove a fireplace, bear in mind the points discussed in the following sections.

Home Improvements that Add Value to Your Home

Once you have moved into your first home, you will be tempted to try and turn it into a palace. Aside from the cost of home improvement, you could find that you lose out in other ways. Mock tudor beams in your modern flat may be your idea of great design, but you are likely to find that they reduce the potential value of your home when you come to sell. As a first-time buyer you are likely to move on within three to five years, so you should ask yourself:

▌ Is it worth spending all this money on improvements, when I am going to move in a few years?

▌ Will the £10,000 kitchen I am buying add £10,000 to the value of the property?

▌ Are the decorations/improvements I am planning likely to appeal to buyers when I come to sell my home or will they put buyers off?

Most expensive home improvements do not add a corresponding value to your property, but they can add 'saleability' by improving your chances of getting a quick sale at or near the asking price.

Central heating systems and garages are the most likely to add more in value than they cost to install. Extra bedrooms also boost the value of a property.

You should concentrate on the kitchen and bathroom and keeping the property in good decorative order – simple and tasteful. These are the things to bear in mind:

▌ A good quality kitchen is important. But it does not have to be expensive. You can make the most of your existing kitchen by changing the cupboard doors and worktops or by retiling.

▌ If you need extra space a loft conversion is an option. However, £10,000 spent will generally add only £4000 to the value of the property. Also be aware that it will affect the appearance of the property, and if it is not in keeping with others in the street, could adversely affect its value.

▌ A separate toilet (even if it is tucked away under the stairs and it doubles as a cloakroom) adds value and can be relatively inexpensive. But don't compromise on valuable living or bedroom space.

▌ Don't get rid of original features such as cornicing, wood panelling or fireplaces, and if they have been removed consider replacing them with originals from a reclamation yard. A period property with original or sympathetically restored features can often achieve 5 to 15 per cent more than properties with none of these features. Double glazing rarely recoups its cost on sale and on period properties properly restored sash windows are more appealing to buyers than modern aluminium ones.

▌ Extensions usually require planning permission and should be in sympathy with the style of your property. And conservatories, while adding extra room, may also add less value than the cost of building one. Be aware of compromising garden space.

▌ Often cheaper improvements add more value – a new front door or better lighting.

▌ A power shower (rather than expensive instalments such as a jacuzzi) will add value and save on your hot water bills.

▌ Don't knock down walls unless you have to. It can reduce the value of your home (fewer rooms generally mean a lower price) unless you have plenty of space. If you want to give the illusion of more room, an arch with sliding or double doors may be a better option.

▌ Wood flooring is popular and can be inexpensive if you have existing floorboards. You can strip, sand and varnish the floorboards yourself and should find this cheaper than having wall-to-wall carpets fitted.

▌ Taste is very subjective. Avocado bathroom suites and swirly brown carpets may come back into vogue, but it is better to stick to white in the bathroom and plain carpets if you want to ensure the maximum value of your property when you come to sell.

Major Works

If you need to start major building work, always contact your local council planning department for permission. In a conservation area there are likely to be restrictions on any work that will affect the appearance and character of the property. All new building work must conform to building regulations. Council building-control officers are entitled to inspect work and charge a fee for approving it.

If you live in a terraced or semi-detached house and undertake work that affects the party wall you normally need written agreement from your neighbours.

Building work almost always costs far more than you expect. So before starting work bear in mind the following:

▌ Obtain realistic quotes – don't always go for the cheapest if that means cutting corners, the quote could be increased halfway through work or, because the work becomes uneconomic for the builder, he takes on other work and yours takes far longer than expected.

▌ Get fixed prices if possible and do not agree hourly or daily rates as these are incentives for the builder to spend longer on the job.

▌ Consider employing an architect if you want an extension or major work. A chartered surveyor can be employed for smaller alterations.

For advice on choosing an architect contact the advisory services of:

The Royal Institute of British Architects: 020 7307 3700
Royal Incorporation of Architects in Scotland: 0131 229 7205
Royal Institute of the Architects of Ireland: 00 3531 676 1703

For advice on choosing a surveyor contact the advisory services of:

The Royal Institution of Chartered Surveyors: 020 7222 7000
The Royal Institution of Chartered Surveyors in Scotland:
0131 225 7078
The Association of Building Engineers: 01604 404121
The Architects and Surveyors Institute: 01249 444505

Do not change your mind once you have agreed on what work will be done. Any changes to the contract or extra works are normally charged at a higher rate. Allow for contingencies such as the discovery of damp or woodrot.

Employing a Builder

We have all heard horror stories about builders taking three times as long as expected to complete work, charging five times as much as agreed or disappearing half way through a job. Employing a builder is bound to be stressful – even if you pick a good one. You will have workmen in your home, they will create dust and you will get fed up with the fact that they keep drinking your tea or arrive while you are still in bed.

To minimize the stress follow these tips:

▌ Where possible, employ a builder/electrician/handyman who has been recommended to you – ask your neighbours, the estate agent, etc.

▌ Pick a builder/electrician/workman who is a member of a trade body such as The Federation of Master Builders or who is listed in the National Register of Warranted Builders (and as such is bound by a code of practice and offers a warranty for any defects arising from faulty workmanship or materials within the first two years). The telephone numbers for these are 020 7242 7583 and 020 7404 4155 respectively. The Construction Confederation (020 7608 5000) can also supply a list of member firms (it offers a guarantee scheme).

▌ Get estimates from two or three builders and make sure you ask them to quote for exactly the same work by typing out a specification list.

▌ Make sure that any contracts you sign are specific and write in any additional clauses you think are necessary.

▌ Be wary of paying money in advance. Stage payments – with a small amount up-front and then payments as each stage of the work is completed – will protect you should the builder runoff with your money and give an incentive for the builder to complete works quickly.

▌ Think twice about paying cash in hand so the builder can avoid VAT and tax. Not only will this mean you do not get a guarantee or warranty, but you may find it difficult to pursue your case in the courts if the building work is shoddy – or worse, half your home is demolished because you have employed a cowboy.

Employing an Electrician

Contact the National Inspection Council for Electrical Installation Contracting for a list of approved electrical contractors (020 7582 7746) or the Electrical Contractors Association for lists of members (020 7229 1266 or 0131 445 5577 in Scotland).

Employing a Plumber

The Institute of Plumbing has a register of plumbers which is monitored by the British Standards Institution (01708 472791).

Do-It-Yourself

As a first-time buyer you may not have enough cash to pay for someone else to do work for you. Only undertake jobs that mean you will make savings. In some cases it can be cheaper to employ a professional who can not only complete the work to a higher standard and more quickly, but can buy materials at trade prices. Before starting:

▌ Make sure you can complete the work and will not have to pay a builder to complete it for you – or worse to repair any damage you have done.

▌ Buy materials at wholesalers or trade outlets if possible. You will find the costs are much lower.

▌ Don't tackle anything for which you are not qualified, espe-
cially anything to do with electricity or gas (only qualified gas
fitters are allowed to connect a gas supply to an appliance).

▌ To cut costs and make work easier, consider hiring the equipment professionals use.

14 Once You Have Moved In

Reducing Your Household Bills

It is only when you become a property owner, that you realize how much running a home actually costs. To keep your bills to the minimum consider the following.

Council Tax

One of the few times that you can challenge your council tax valuation is after you move into a property. But be careful that the valuations tribunal does not put your home into a higher council tax band.

Water Metering

It usually pays only to have a water meter installed if you have a high rateable value and low consumption.

Gas

The deregulation of the gas market means that some 19 million consumers can shop around for the cheapest deal. You will still have the same gas supplied via the existing pipes and meter. The only difference is who sells you the gas and sends the bill. Watch out for the small print if you plan to switch companies. You will have to sign a binding contract. Prices will depend on how much gas you use and how you pay, with a discount for those who pay by direct debit. Compare the standing charge as well as the price per unit. Some suppliers offer incentives such as cash backs, price discounts or money-off vouchers. If you sign a fixed contract you will normally have to pay a fee if you want to cancel the contract early.

The average gas bill of £260 can be cut by 10 per cent or more by shopping around. The savings on a three-bedroom house can be as much as £100.

Telephone

You will probably spend between £200 and £300 a year on your telephone bill – if not more. Although it may not seem worthwhile switching phone services to save £50 or so a year, over the long run savings do mount up.

In some cases you will be better off using an alternative to BT. The annual rental of a BT phone is over £100 – almost double the cheapest line rental from a cable company.

If your area has cable television you may find that by switching to a cable telephone service you can cut your bills substantially. The Cable Information Service on 0990 111 777 will tell you if your area has a cable service. Radio-based home telephone companies are another alternative. In Scotland, Atlantic offers such a service.

If you decide to stick with BT, sign up for discount schemes. The most obvious one is BT Friends and Family, which gives a discount of 10 per cent on calls made to ten telephone numbers that you select. You can select one mobile phone and one international telephone number. If you combine this service with other residential customer discount schemes, the savings can be up to 25 per cent.

Even if your phone bill is very low you can make savings. Sign up for the Light User scheme, which provides a rebate for those making very few calls of up to 60 per cent.

By simply paying your phone bill by direct debit you will receive a £1 rebate on your quarterly line rental charge.

Those who run up larger phone bills can make savings by joining the Premierline service. Although (at the time of going to press) it costs £24 a year or £6 a quarter if you spend more than £70 a quarter on phone calls (excluding line rental) you can make savings of around £15 on a £100 total phone bill.

You can use indirect access phone companies for some calls and continue to make local calls using BT. Mercury, Dial 1602 and ACC all offer these services, but they will only appeal to those who make a large number of long national calls or regular international calls.

Remember that, although some alternative telephone companies offer a saving of more than 20 per cent on international or other calls, you will have to pay either a line rental or a quarterly fee.

The Consumers' Association recently calculated that you can pay more than £6 or less than 60p for a five-minute call to the USA, depending on the service you use. The cheapest way to access these calls is through an international call reseller, which can be accessed from any touch tone phone. However, you must first open an account with the company, so it will not be an option for those who make only occasional international calls.

Electricity/Fuel Bills

There are several ways in which you can cut your gas and electricity bills:

1 Install low-energy, long-life lightbulbs. They may be more expensive to buy, but over a year you can save up to £10 per bulb, or up to £60 in the bulb's lifetime of up to five years.
2 Draught proof windows and doors (you can do it yourself) to save up to £20 a year. Lining curtains with a thermal material and keeping them drawn as much as possible will also conserve heat.
3 Lag your hot water tank, if it is not already lagged, or buy an additional one so the jacket is at least 80 mm thick. The savings are up to £10 a year.
4 Make the most of thermostatic radiator valves to regulate the temperature of radiators – the flow of hot water is reduced once the thermostat reaches a set temperature.
5 If you live in a house, adequate loft insulation of at least 150 mm is recommended, but remember to lag pipes in the roof space to stop them freezing and to insulate your water tank.
6 Turn down your central heating thermostat by 1 degree – there will be very little difference in temperature – and savings can be up to 10 per cent.

7   Don't leave electrical items switched on or on standby unless you need to. A TV can use up to one-third as much power when it's on standby as when it's actually on.

8   If you live in a house built after 1930 and don't already have cavity wall insulation it should be considered. It can be expensive (around £600), but the savings can be up to a quarter of the price each year.

9   If you have your hot water and central heating on timer switches make sure these are used effectively and do not heat up the house or water when not necessary.

10   If you have a fireplace that you don't use, consider blocking it up (don't forget the air brick for adequate ventilation).

For further information contact your local electricity company. Most have energy efficiency teams that give free advice on energy saving.

Insurance

As discussed earlier, it pays to shop around for insurance. Remember, that just because a company is the cheapest this year, it may not be next year.

Mortgage

If, after moving into your new home, you find that you could have taken out a much cheaper mortgage with another lender you can switch your home loan. But remember:

▌ Some cheap mortgages are only offered to first-time buyers and you are no longer a first-time buyer.

▌ If you have taken out a low-start, discount, fixed rate or capped mortgage you may have to pay redemption penalties of several thousand pounds if you switch your mortgage in the first one to five years.

▌ If you take out another mortgage you may be required to switch your endowment policy and, as such, could lose all of the premiums you have already paid.

▌ Even if you have to pay redemption penalties you may still be better off switching your mortgage if the savings outweigh the additional costs.

Direct Debits

If you pay your electricity, telephone and other bills by direct debit you will usually qualify for lower payments.

Dealing with Leaseholder Problems

If you have bought a leasehold flat or house, you may find that the freeholder fails to maintain the property or that you want to extend your lease or to buy the freehold.

Problems with the Freeholder/Management Company

Under the 1993 Leasehold Reform, Housing and Urban Development Act, leaseholders have the right to a management audit and can appoint a surveyor to make sure the property is being managed properly.

If you have a complaint about service charges, insurance, the cost or quality of any building works or the quality of the management of the block/building you can now take your case to a Leasehold Valuation Tribunal. These can settle disputes and, as a last resort, can appoint new managers to run blocks of flats. The Department of Environment, Transport and the Regions has a free booklet called *Applying to a Leasehold Valuation Tribunal* – call 0870 122 6236 for a copy.

As with any dispute, you should make sure you put all your complaints in writing and keep copies of all correspondence. Make sure you have the support of fellow leaseholders, as this will strengthen your case.

Buying the Freehold/Extending the Lease

Under the Leasehold Reform, Housing and Urban Development Act 1993 you may be able to buy the freehold of your property or join together with others in your block of flats to purchase the freehold. To qualify:

▌ the lease must have originally been for over 21 years

▌ you must have a low rent (£1000 in London or £250 elsewhere; or less than two-thirds of the rateable value; or the rent in the first year must be less than two-thirds of the letting value)

▌ and you must have lived in the property as your only or principal residence for the previous three years or three years out of the last ten.

For collective enfranchisement (when flat owners club together to purchase the freehold):

▌ the property must have two or more flats held by qualifying tenants

▌ if the building was not purpose built as flats and has less than five flats it must not have a resident landlord

▌ it must be in a single freehold ownership

▌ the property must not include more than 10 per cent of non-residential floor space

▌ at least two-thirds of the flats must be held by qualifying tenants

▌ at least two-thirds of qualifying tenants (half the total number of flats) must wish to participate and must occupy their flat as their principal or only residence and must have done so for the preceding year or for three years out of the previous ten.

In addition, qualifying lessees can buy a 90-year lease extension, provided that they can meet the residence requirements. Remember, if you are buying a flat with the aim of buying the freehold you will have to be a resident for at least a year (but often three years), you will have to ensure that other lessees are equally determined and will find the procedures complex and costly (including paying both sides' fees).

The other option is where the landlord intends to sell the freehold. In this case, tenants must be given right of first refusal to buy at that price. In this case the landlord's costs do not have to be met and there are fewer restrictions on the tenants who qualify.

However, you may be able to improve the value of your flat by opting for the simpler route of a 90-year lease extension. For a start this can be done independently of other lessees. However, if you and other lessees are unhappy with the management of the building you may still want to opt for the more difficult and costly alternative of buying the freehold.

Problems Paying the Mortgage

As discussed in the chapter on mortgages, homebuyers are now advised to take out mortgage protection insurance to cover their mortgage repayments should they be unable to work due to ill health or redundancy.

Insurance currently costs around £5 for every £100 of monthly repayment covered and is worth buying because:

▌ renters who lose their jobs can often get housing benefit if their partner is still in work, but homebuyers must struggle on one salary as they receive no benefit if one partner is working

▌ new buyers (those who bought since October 1995) get no state help with their mortgage for the first nine months if they lose their job and claim Income Support (renters get help to pay their rent almost immediately)

The Council of Mortgage Lenders has now proposed that this insurance is made compulsory and the government is now considering this.

As you are unlikely to get state help to pay your mortgage, and if you have no insurance, you will find that you quickly fall into arrears and risk repossession. To minimize the risks:

- Contact your mortgage lender as soon as you lose your job/find it difficult to meet your monthly mortgage repayments.

- Ask if you can reduce or defer mortgage payments until you find a new job/sort out your finances. Lenders will normally only agree to this if you have sufficient equity in your property. If your mortgage is worth almost as much as the value of your property the lender may feel that there is a risk that, if you sell your home or it is repossessed, the sale proceeds may not cover the outstanding mortgage debt.

- Contact your local Citizens Advice Bureau for advice on dealing with creditors.

- Keep your mortgage lender informed of any changes in your circumstances and your attempts to find another job.

- Find out if you can rent the property for more than your monthly mortgage bills and ask your lender if it will agree to you renting out the property to cover the costs.

- Try to pay at least some of the mortgage repayments – even if you have to take a temporary job and rent out a room to do so.

- Avoid repossession at all costs. It will be better for you to sell the property than for it to be repossessed because:

    – if you sell the property yourself you are likely to receive a higher sale price than would be achieved if the property were sold after repossession (when it may have been left empty for several months)

– if you sell the property yourself you will not be credit blacklisted – if it is repossessed you will find it difficult to take out another mortgage at a future date

Your mortgage lender will have to agree to the sale so discuss your plans before putting the property on the market. If you are in negative equity – the value of your property is less than your outstanding mortgage debt – you will have to prove you can repay the balance in order to get the agreement of your lender to sell the property.

▋ If you are taken to court for non-payment of your mortgage always attend the hearing and fight your case. You may be able to delay repossession for long enough to find another job.

Wills

Now that you are a homeowner it is important for you to draw up a will or amend your existing one. This is particularly important if you have jointly purchased the property (see joint ownership on page 51).

Two-thirds of people die without making a valid will, and yet the implications of failing to do so can be devastating. Your estranged parents, or brothers and sisters you never speak to, can receive all your estate or, worse, the person with whom you are cohabiting may not inherit the property, even though this is what you intend.

The rules of intestacy (if you fail to make a will) specify that your inheritance is split between your surviving spouse and children – if you are unmarried and childless, other relatives then inherit your estate. The rules vary depending on whether you come under English, Scottish or Northern Irish rules.

Drawing Up a Will

Even if you seek professional advice in drawing up a will you must make sure that it is drawn up correctly and meets your wishes. A recent *Which?* survey found that 15 out of 51 wills were poorly drawn up, and in some cases those designed to inherit may have been unable to because of confusing wording. And make sure your will covers all eventualities. For instance, if you leave a certain possession to a friend, what happens if he or she dies before you? The problem is that you will not know if your will is inadequate until it is too late.

Be wary of appointing a professional executor at the time of will writing as some of the banks can charge high fees for dealing with your will, and these can substantially reduce the value of your estate.

You can either approach a solicitor, bank, building society or life insurance company or a specialist will writing company. Will writers are members of one of the following trade bodies: the Society of Will Writers, the Willwriters Association and the Institute of Professional Willwriters. They do regulate their members, but do not have compensation schemes.

If the will is not drawn up properly it could be invalid and the rules of intestacy could apply. So if the will does not specify what happens if the main beneficiary dies before you, the will could be invalid.

Once you have drawn up a will you should review it regularly so it reflects any changes in your circumstances.

You will also need to appoint one or two executors (these can be friends or family) to administer your will on behalf of the beneficiaries.

Finally, store your will in a safe place – preferably with a third party – where it can be easily found by your executors.

Appendix: Monthly Mortgage Costs

Interest Rate	Amount of Mortgage	REPAYMENT		ENDOWMENT	
		10% MIRAS	No MIRAS	10% MIRAS	No MIRAS
3%	£40,000.00	£183.93	£191.43	£92.50	£100.00
	£50,000.00	£231.78	£239.28	£117.50	£125.00
	£60,000.00	£279.64	£287.14	£142.50	£150.00
	£80,000.00	£375.35	£382.85	£192.50	£200.00
	£100,000.00	£471.07	£478.57	£242.50	£250.00
	£150,000.00	£710.35	£717.85	£367.50	£375.00
4%	£40,000.00	£203.37	£213.37	£123.34	£133.34
	£50,000.00	£256.72	£266.72	£156.67	£166.67
	£60,000.00	£310.06	£320.06	£190.00	£200.00
	£80,000.00	£416.75	£426.75	£256.67	£266.67
	£100,000.00	£523.43	£533.43	£323.34	£333.34
	£150,000.00	£790.15	£800.15	£490.00	£500.00
5%	£40,000.00	£224.01	£236.51	£154.17	£166.67
	£50,000.00	£283.13	£295.64	£195.84	£208.34
	£60,000.00	£342.26	£354.76	£237.50	£250.00
	£80,000.00	£460.52	£473.02	£320.84	£333.34
	£100,000.00	£578.77	£591.27	£404.17	£416.67
	£150,000.00	£874.40	£886.91	£612.50	£625.00
6%	£40,000.00	£245.76	£260.76	£185.00	£200.00
	£50,000.00	£310.95	£325.94	£235.00	£250.00
	£60,000.00	£376.14	£391.13	£285.00	£300.00
	£80,000.00	£506.51	£521.51	£385.00	£400.00
	£100,000.00	£636.89	£651.89	£485.00	£500.00
	£150,000.00	£962.84	£977.83	£735.00	£750.00
7%	£40,000.00	£268.54	£286.04	£215.84	£233.34
	£50,000.00	£340.05	£357.54	£274.17	£291.67
	£60,000.00	£411.56	£429.05	£332.50	£350.00

	£80,000.00	£554.57	£572.07	£449.17	£466.67
	£100,000.00	£697.59	£715.09	£565.84	£583.34
	£150,000.00	£1,055.14	£1,072.63	£857.50	£875.00
8%	£40,000.00	£292.27	£312.26	£246.67	£266.67
	£50,000.00	£370.33	£390.33	£313.34	£333.34
	£60,000.00	£448.40	£468.39	£380.00	£400.00
	£80,000.00	£604.53	£624.53	£513.34	£533.34
	£100,000.00	£760.66	£780.66	£646.67	£666.67
	£150,000.00	£1,150.99	£1,170.98	£980.00	£1,000.00
9%	£40,000.00	£316.86	£339.35	£277.50	£300.00
	£50,000.00	£401.70	£424.19	£352.50	£375.00
	£60,000.00	£486.54	£509.03	£427.50	£450.00
	£80,000.00	£656.21	£678.71	£577.50	£600.00
	£100,000.00	£825.89	£848.39	£727.50	£750.00
	£150,000.00	£1,250.08	£1,272.58	£1,102.50	£1,125.00
10%	£40,000.00	£342.23	£367.23	£308.34	£333.34
	£50,000.00	£434.03	£459.03	£391.67	£416.67
	£60,000.00	£525.84	£550.84	£475.00	£500.00
	£80,000.00	£709.45	£734.45	£641.67	£666.67
	£100,000.00	£893.07	£918.07	£808.34	£833.34
	£150,000.00	£1,352.10	£1,377.10	£1,225.00	£1,250.00
11%	£40,000.00	£368.30	£395.80	£339.17	£366.67
	£50,000.00	£467.25	£494.75	£430.84	£458.34
	£60,000.00	£566.20	£593.70	£522.50	£550.00
	£80,000.00	£764.10	£791.60	£705.84	£733.34
	£100,000.00	£962.00	£989.50	£889.17	£916.67
	£150,000.00	£1,456.75	£1,484.25	£1,347.50	£1,375.00
12%	£40,000.00	£395.00	£425.00	£370.00	£400.00
	£50,000.00	£501.25	£531.25	£470.00	£500.00
	£60,000.00	£607.50	£637.50	£570.00	£600.00
	£80,000.00	£820.00	£850.00	£770.00	£800.00
	£100,000.00	£1,032.50	£1,062.50	£970.00	£1,000.00
	£150,000.00	£1,563.75	£1,593.75	£1,470.00	£1,500.00
13%	£40,000.00	£422.25	£454.75	£400.84	£433.34
	£50,000.00	£535.94	£568.44	£509.17	£541.67
	£60,000.00	£649.62	£682.13	£617.50	£650.00
	£80,000.00	£877.00	£909.51	£834.17	£866.67
	£100,000.00	£1,104.38	£1,136.88	£1,050.84	£1,083.34
	£150,000.00	£1,672.82	£1,705.32	£1,592.50	£1,625.00

Assumes a 25 year mortgage term and that the tax relief ceiling is £30,000. Payments exclude life insurance and endowment premiums. Payment figures assume the mortgage qualifies for MIRAS (mortgage interest tax relief at source). This rate of tax relief is currently 10 per cent on the first £30,000 of your mortgage. Tax relief will be scrapped from April 2000.

Source: Halifax plc

The Daily Telegraph

Guide to Funerals and Bereavement

Sam Weller

Funerals are probably one of the largest yet most unexpected costs that we have to face, yet arranging a funeral usually takes place when the bereaved are at their most vulnerable. Unfortunately, the funeral directing trade is not licensed or regulated and there is concern about the level of pricing and standards. Relatives do not wish to appear mean where their loved ones are concerned so often end up paying more than they can afford.

In this practical book Sam Weller examines the entire 'death care industry'. He provides clear information on arranging a funeral, cremation, burial and memorialization, and the costs involved. He takes a holistic view of death and its aftermath. The book spans:

- **planning for a funeral and what to do when someone dies**
- **memorialization**
- **ownership and inheritance of grave plots**
- **rights and responsibilities in cemeteries and churchyards.**

£8.99 • Paperback • ISBN 0 7494 3057 5 • 208 pages • 1999

KOGAN PAGE
120 Pentonville Road, London N1 9JN
Tel: 0171 278 0433 • Fax: 0171 837 6348 • w w w . k o g a n - p a g e . c o . u k

Index

Index of Advertisers